THE ISMS: MODERN DOCTRINES AND MOVEMENTS

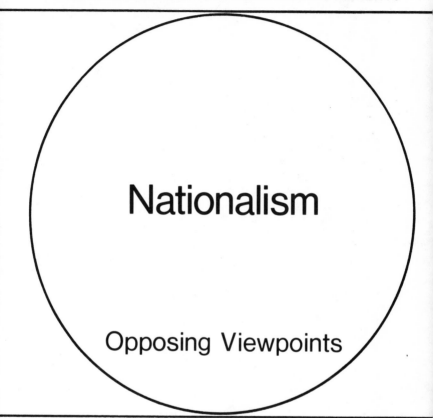

Nationalism

Opposing Viewpoints

Bruno Leone

GREENHAVEN PRESS, INC.
1611 POLK ST. N.E.
MINNEAPOLIS, MINNESOTA 55413

SERIES EDITORS: DAVID L. BENDER AND GARY E. McCUEN

© Copyright 1978 by Greenhaven Press, Inc.

ISBN 0-912616-56-3 Paper Edition
ISBN 0-912616-57-1 Cloth Edition

Nationalism

Contents

Nationalism

Preface

In his compelling essay, ''The Duties of Man,'' the nineteenth century Italian patriot Giuseppe Mazzini wrote:

> O my Brothers! love your country. Our country is our home, the home which God has given us, placing therein a numerous family which we love and are loved by, and with which we have a more intimate and quicker communion of feeling and thought than with others; a family which by its concentration upon a given spot, and by the homogeneous nature of its elements, is destined for a special kind of activity.

Emotional and farseeing, Mazzini's sentiments were expressive of nationalism, the principal force shaping nineteenth century European and twentieth century world civilization.

Modern nationalism began as a liberal reaction to the autocracy of the dynastic states of Europe. Before the nineteenth century, nationality was based upon personal allegiance to a monarch. Thus a Frenchman living in 1785 would rightfully consider himself a subject of the Bourbon King Louis XVI rather than a citizen of France. Moreover, the Frenchman need not even have been French by language and tradition as most of the dynastic states were made up of a mixture (often hostile to each other) of culturally diverse peoples.

During the first half of the nineteenth century, however, the idea of allegiance to a geographical nation (not an individual) composed of people joined by language, custom, and a common historical tradition proved too seductive to resist. Inspired by nationalistic writers like Jean Paul Marat in France, Guiseppe Mazzini in Italy and Johann Wolfgang von Goethe in Germany, one by one the states of Europe underwent a change which was more than cosmetic as governments and national boundaries were reforged along the logical lines of cultural distinctiveness. In France, Louis XVI was dethroned,

1

eventually beheaded, and the monarchy replaced by a Republican form of government. Germany, which at one time was composed of over three hundred independent principalities, was moving toward unification under the leadership of Prussia, the most powerful of the independent German states. Italy was following a path similar to Germany as Italian nationalists sought to unite their homeland while ridding it of foreign rule. The Balkan states of Europe aspired to free themselves from the domination of the Ottoman Turks, a domination which had lasted over three hundred years.

Nor were unification and freedom from foreign and dynastic rule the sole or primary aims of early nationalism. The far more blessed goal of a free constitution under which individual rights supplanted governmental despotism was considered of even greater consequence. In fact, the promise of personal liberty and the general advancement of the material well-being of an enlightened citizenry were the motive factors underlying the nationalistic movements of the first half of the nineteenth century.

Finally, the lofty prospects of peace, cooperation and brotherhood among the free and newly emergent states of Europe were added adornments. The relationship of peoples both within and between states would be governed by humanitarian principles. Indeed, a liberal cocoon appeared to be enveloping the map and temperament of Europe.

But by the middle of the century, the character of nationalism experienced a fundamental change. As the cocoon broke open, in lieu of the promised harmony, the monster of chauvinism showed its ugly head. Humanitarianism was replaced by aggression, the exhaltation of the individual by the exhaltation of the state. Whereas the state at first was considered the means to achieve a cherished end, the state now became an end in itself, an organic unity which enjoyed an existence exclusive of those residing within its borders.

And another powerful and more ominous feature of this ''new'' nationalism was its expansionist tendency. The old nationalism aspired to unify the nation — one nation in one state and little else. The new nationalism sanctioned the imposition of one nation's values and standards upon another. All was fair game in the arena of international politics, territorial expansion included. The imperialistic totalitarian movements of the twentieth century were the logical termination of this aggressive brand of nationalism.

Since its impact first was felt in nineteenth century Europe, nationalism has been an irrepressible force which has left (and continues to leave) its peculiar imprint upon the course of history. Yet as a shaping force in world civilization, nationalism can be either beneficial or destructive, depending upon how it is used. When governments advocate international assistance, tolerance and fellowship without necessarily sacrificing the national distinctiveness with which a people may identify and grow, nationalism can be a constructive force. Conversely, when exclusivism is preached and imperialism practiced, nationalism can be the most divisive and potentially the most catastrophic force in the history of humankind.

Chapter 1

Nationalism

Nineteenth Century Nationalism:
The "Old" and the "New"

INTRODUCTION

Perhaps no nineteenth century thinkers better typify the
contrast between the "old" and the "new" nationalism than
Guiseppe Mazzini and Heinrich von Treitschke. Although both
were ardent nationalists, the similarities ended there. Mazzini
was a high principled moralist who advocated harmony and
cooperation between nations; Von Trietschke was an amoral
Machiavellian who condoned self-serving militarism. Mazzini
regarded offensive warfare as a sin against God and man; Von
Trietschke viewed all warfare as a "sacred" rite of purification
in which "the chaff is winnowed from the wheat." Mazzini
preached that the state derived its just powers from the people;
Von Trietschke held the reverse to be true. As the following
readings will illustrate, even the tone and style of their works
highlight their differences. Mazzini is passionate, emotional
and high-sounding, while von Trietschke always remains
controlled, detached and direct.

The readings by Gladstone and Rohrbach are also illustrative of
the "old" versus the "new" nationalism. A prophet of nineteenth century liberalism, Gladstone was convinced that the
advancement of European civilization would be realized only if
the spirit of brotherhood existed among peoples and states.
Conversely, the jingoistic Rohrbach believed that the mission
and destiny of Germany should take precedent over such
visionary fancies as a fellowship of European nations.

Nationalism: The Exhaltation of the Individual

Giuseppe Mazzini

Guiseppe Mazzini (1805-1872) was the founder of *Biovine Italia* (Young Italy), a movement which advocated the independence and unification of Italy under a Republican form of government. A humanitarian and internationalist, he also founded *Giovine Europa* (Young Europe) in hopes of uniting all Europe into a brotherhood of free peoples. Mazzini was a persevering and dauntless patriot who was sentenced to death three times for participating in revolutions aimed at unifying Italy.

Consider the following questions while reading:

1. What does Mazzini say are one's duties to humanity?
2. What is the purpose of the nation?

From **The Duties of Man, and Other Essays** by Giuseppe Mazzini. An Everyman's Library Edition. Published in the United States by E.P. Dutton, and reprinted with their permission. This reading is taken from pages 51, 52, 54, 55, 59.

DUTIES TO HUMANITY

Your first Duties — first, at least, in importance — are...to Humanity. You are *men* before you are *citizens* or *fathers*. If you do not embrace the whole human family in your love, if you do not confess your faith in its unity — consequent on the unity of God — and in the brotherhood of the Peoples who are appointed to reduce that unity to fact — if wherever one of your fellowmen groans, wherever the dignity of human nature is violated by falsehood or tyranny, you are not prompt, being able, to succour that wretched one, or do not feel yourself called, being able, to fight for the purpose of relieving the deceived or oppressed — you disobey your law of life, or do not comprehend the religion which will bless the future.

DISAPPEARANCE OF BAD GOVERNMENTS

But what can *each* of you, with his isolated powers, *do* for the moral improvement, for the progress of Humanity...? God gave you this means when he gave you a Country, when, like a wise overseer of labour, who distributes the different parts of the work according to the capacity of the workmen, he divided Humanity into distinct groups upon the face of our globe, and thus planted the seeds of nations. Bad governments have disfigured the design of God, which you may see clearly marked out, as far, at least, as regards Europe, by the courses of the great rivers, by the lines of the lofty mountains, and by other geographical conditions; they have disfigured it by conquest, by greed, by jealousy of the just sovereignty of others; disfigured it so much that to-day there is perhaps no nation except England and France whose confines correspond to this design. They did not, and they do not, recognise any country except their own families and dynasties, the egoism of caste. But the divine design will infallibly be fulfilled. Natural divisions, the innate spontaneous tendencies of the peoples will replace the arbitrary divisions sanctioned by bad governments. The map of Europe will be remade. The Countries of the People will rise, defined by the voice of the free, upon the ruins of the Countries of Kings and privileged castes. Between these Countries there will be harmony and brotherhood. And then the work of Humanity for the general amelioration, for the discovery and application of the real law of life, carried on in association and distributed according to local capacities, will be accomplished by peaceful and progressive development; then each of you, strong in the affections and in the aid of many millions of men speaking the same language, endowed with the same tendencies, and educated by the same historic tradition, may hope by your personal effort to benefit the whole of Humanity....

THE AIM OF GOVERNMENT

The ultimate aim of government is not to rule, nor to restrain by fear, nor to exact obedience, but contrariwise, to free every man from fear, that he may live in all possible security.

Baruch Spinoza (1632 - 1677)

Italy Before Unification

PURPOSE OF THE NATION

[Italy] is our home, the home which God has given us, placing therein a numerous family which we love and are loved by, and with which we have a more intimate and quicker communion of feeling and thought than with others; a family which by its concentration upon a given spot, and by the homogeneous nature of its elements, is destined for a special kind of activity. Our Country is our field of labour; the products of our activity must go forth from it for the benefit of the whole earth; but the instruments of labour which we can use best and most effectively exist in it, and we may not reject them without being unfaithful to God's purpose and diminishing our own strength. In labouring according to true principles for our Country we are labouring for Humanity; our Country is the fulcrum of the lever which we have to wield for the common good. If we give up this fulcrum we run the risk of becoming useless to our Country and to Humanity. Before *associating* ourselves with the Nations which compose Humanity we must exist as a Nation. There can be no association except among equals; and you have no recognized collective existence.

GOD-GIVEN DUTIES

Humanity is a great army moving to the conquest of unknown lands, against powerful and wary enemies. The Peoples are the different corps and divisions of that army. Each has a post entrusted to it; each a special operation to perform; and the common victory depends on the exactness with which the different operations are carried out. Do not disturb the order of the battle. Do not abandon the banner which God has given you. Wherever you may be, into the midst of whatever people circumstances may have driven you, fight for the liberty of that people if the moment calls for it; but fight as Italians, so that the blood which you shed may win honour and love, not for you only, but for your Country. And may the constant thought of your soul be for Italy, may all the acts of your life be worthy of her, and may the standard beneath which you range yourselves to work for Humanity be Italy's. Do not say *I*; say *we*. Be every one of you an incarnation of your Country, and feel himself and make himself responsible for his fellow-countrymen; let each one of you learn to act in such a way that in him men shall respect and love his Country....

9

Nationalism: The Exhaltation of the State

Heinrich von Treitschke

A professor of history at the University of Berlin, Heinrich von Treitschke (1834-1896) was one of Germany's most articulate and fervent nationalistic spokesmen. He perceived the State to be an organic entity to whose will the citizenry should respond with a slavish obedience. Without the State, man loses his *raison d'etre* (reason for being). Von Treitschke believed that the German nation of his day was on the threshold of a glorious political hegemony and he demanded the myopic loyalty of its people. The nationalistic, anti-semitic and antiliberal bias which distinguish his works, clearly earmark him as an intellectual forerunner of twentieth century Nazism.

Consider the following questions while reading:

1. How does Von Treitschke define the power of the state?
2. What services does the State provide?
3. Why is war essential for a nation?
4. Why is blind loyalty to the State a virtue?

Heinrich von Treitschka, **Politics, Volume I** (New York: Macmillan, 1916), pp. 3, 14-16, 19, 22-24, 26, 29, 64-67, 79.

THE STATE IS THE ULTIMATE POWER

The rational task of a legally constituted people, conscious of a destiny, is to assert its rank in the world's hierarchy and in its measure to participate in the great civilizing mission of mankind.

Further, if we examine our definition of the State as "the people legally united as an independent entity," we find that it can be more briefly put thus: "The State is the public force for Offence and Defence...." [It] protects and embraces the people's life, regulating its external aspects on every side. It does not ask primarily for opinion, but demands obedience, and its laws must be obeyed, whether willingly or no....

The State is not an Academy of Arts. If it neglects its strength in order to promote the idealistic aspirations of man, it repudiates its own nature and perishes. This is in truth for the State equivalent to the sin against the Holy Ghost, for it is indeed a mortal error in the State to subordinate itself for sentimental reasons to a foreign Power, as we Germans have often done to England....

We have described the State as an independent force. This pregnant theory of independence implies firstly so absolute a moral supremacy that the State cannot legitimately tolerate any power above its own, and secondly a temporal freedom entailing a variety of material resources adequate to its protection against hostile influences. Legal sovereignty, the State's complete independence of any other earthly power, is so rooted in its nature that it may be said to be its very standard and criterion....

WAR IS ESSENTIAL FOR THE STATE

It is clear that the international agreements which limit the power of a State are not absolute, but voluntary self-restrictions. Hence, it follows that the establishment of a permanent international Arbitration Court is incompatible with the nature of the State, which could at all events only accept the decision of such a tribunal in cases of second- or third-rate importance. When a nation's existence is at stake there is no outside Power whose impartiality can be trusted....It is, moreover, a point of honour for a State to solve such difficulties for itself. International treaties may indeed become more frequent, but a

11

finally decisive tribunal of the nations is an impossibility. The appeal to arms will be valid until the end of history, and therein lies the sacredness of war....

[An] essential function of the State is the conduct of war....

Without war no State could be. All those we know of arose through war, and the protection of their members by armed force remains their primary and essential task. War, therefore, will endure to the end of history, as long as there is multiplicity of States. The laws of human thought and of human nature forbid any alternative, neither is one to be wished for. The blind worshipper of an eternal peace falls into the error of isolating the State, or dreams of one which is universal, which we have already seen to be at variance with reason.

Even as it is impossible to conceive of a tribunal above the State, which we have recognized as sovereign in its very essence, so it is likewise impossible to banish the idea of war from the world....

THE STATE IS SUPREME

It must be further understood that all the worth which the human being possesses — all spiritual reality — he possesses only through the State....The State is embodied Morality. It is the ethical spirit which has clarified itself and has taken substantial shape as Will....The State is Mind....The State, being an end in itself, is provided with the maximum of rights against the individual citizens, whose highest duty it is to be members of the State....

Georg Wilhelm Friedrich Hegel, **Philosophy of History**

WAR PROVIDES NEEDED HEROES

The grandeur of war lies in the utter annihilation of puny man in the great conception of the State, and it brings out the full magnificence of the sacrifice of fellow-countrymen for one another. In war the chaff is winnowed from the wheat....

It is war which fosters the political idealism which the material-ist rejects. What a disaster for civilization it would be if mankind blotted its heroes from memory. The heroes of a nation are the figures which rejoice and inspire the spirit of its youth, and the writers whose words ring like trumpet blasts become the idols of our boyhood and our early manhood. He who feels no answering thrill is unworthy to bear arms for his country. To appeal from this judgment to Christianity would be sheer perversity, for does not the Bible distinctly say that the ruler shall rule by the sword, and again that greater love hath no man than to lay down his life for his friend? To Aryan races, who are before all things courageous, the foolish preaching of everlasting peace has always been vain. They have always been men enough to maintain with the sword what they have attained through the spirit....

GERMAN DEVOTION TO THE STATE

Germany in the nineteenth century has undoubtedly taken the lead in political science, after having followed the foreigner in this domain for two hundred years. The confused course of our history and the repeated violent interruptions which our development has suffered, have at least had the advantage of keeping us from the traditions and prejudices which have so often obscured the political judgment of other peoples.

The complicated functions of our State arise from our place in the world, our history, and our geographical position, all of which enable us to pursue aims which to other nations seem incompatible with each other....

Steadfast loyalty, even though it may be blind, and sometimes politically mischievous, must always remain a proof of the healthy condition of our State and nation.

Europe: A Family of Nations

William Gladstone

A British prime minister and statesman,
William Gladstone (1809-1898) was the leading
figure in the movement for political and social
reform in nineteenth century Britain. He exhibited a sincere and altruistic concern for the
affairs of humankind and often spoke of inject-
ing politics with the spirit of Christ's Sermon on
the Mount. Although he began his public career
as an implacable foe of reform, ironically, he
ended it as one of the principal agents of the
nineteenth century liberal movement.

Consider the following questions while reading:

1. What criticism does Gladstone make of Germany?
2. How should nations act toward each other?
3. What was to be the greatest triumph of Gladstone's time?

William Gladstone, **Gleanings of Past Years** (New York: Charles Scribner's Sons, 1881), pp.
242-43, 248, 256-57.

ADMONITION TO GERMANY

We hear much of the civilisation of the Germans. Let them remember, that Italy has been built up, at least from 1860 onwards, upon the groundwork of the expressed desires of the people of its several portions; that England surrendered the possession of the Ionian Islands in deference to the popular desire, expressed through the representative Chamber, to be united to Greece; that even the Emperor Napoleon took Savoy and Nice under cover of a vote, as to which no one can say that it clearly belied the real public sentiment. This is surely a great advance on the old and cruel practice of treating the population of a civilised European country as mere chattels. Are we to revert to that old practice? Will its revival be in harmony with the feeling, the best feeling, of Europe? Will it conduce to future peace? Can Germany afford, and does she mean, to set herself up above European opinion...?

THE GERMANS ARE RESPONSIBLE

The Germans are responsible for everything that exists today, for the sickliness and stupidity that oppose culture, the neurosis, called nationalism, from which Europe suffers; they have robbed Europe itself of its meaning and its intelligence. They have led it into a blind alley.

Friedrich Nietzsche (1844-1900)

MISERIES OF THIS AGE

Amidst the many additions which this age has contributed to the comfort and happiness of man, it has made some also to his miseries. And among these last is the deplorable discovery of methods by which we can environ peace with many of the worst attributes of war; as, for instance, with its hostility to the regular development of freedom, through the influence of great standing armies, and the prevalence of military ideas; with its hostility to sound and stable government, through crushing taxation, financial embarrassment, and that constant growth of public debt which now, with somewhat rare exceptions, marks the policy of the States of Europe; with the jealous and angry temper, which it kindles between nations; and lastly, with the almost certainty of war itself, as the issue of that state of highly armed preparation, which, we are affectedly told, is the true security for the avoidance of quarrels among men....

In truth the nations of Europe are a family. Some one of them is likely, if not certain, from time to time to be the strongest, either by inherent power or by favouring opportunity. To this strength great influence will attach; and great power over the lot of others. Such influence and power may be abused....

A NEW LAW OF NATIONS

One accomplishment yet remains needful to enable us to hold without envy our free and eminent position. It is that we should do as we would be done by; that we should seek to found a

British Prime Minister William Gladstone warned against the growth of German nationalism.

moral empire upon the confidence of the several peoples, not upon their fears, their passions, or their antipathies. Certain it is that a new law of nations is gradually taking hold of the mind, and coming to sway the practice, of the world; a law which recognises independence, which frowns upon aggression, which favours the pacific, not the bloody settlement of disputes, which aims at permanent and not temporary adjustments; above all, which recognises, as a tribunal of paramount authority, the general judgment of civilised mankind. It has censured the aggression of France; it will censure, if need arise, the greed of Germany.

It is hard for all nations to go astray. Their ecumenical council sits above the partial passions of those, who are misled by interest, and disturbed by quarrel. The greatest triumph of our time, a triumph in a region loftier than that of electricity and steam, will be the enthronement of this idea of Public Right, as the governing idea of European policy; as the common and precious inheritance of all lands, but superior to the passing opinion of any. The foremost among the nations will be that one, which by its conduct shall gradually engender in the mind of the others a fixed belief that it is just.

Germany: A Nation Above Nations

Paul Rohrbach

Paul Rohrbach was an influential German journalist and avid nationalist. In *The German Idea In the World* written prior to World War I (1912), he celebrates the alleged superiority of German culture and advocates a world-wide policy of political expansion.

Consider the following questions while reading:

1. What is the German idea?
2. What should be Germany's role in the world?

Paul Rohrbach, **German World Policies** (New York: Macmillan, 1915), pp. 4-6, 8, 9.

THE GERMAN IDEA

In speaking of the German idea in the world we mean the ideal force of Germanism as a formative power in relation to the present and future happenings of the world. We start very consciously with the conviction that we have been placed in the arena of the world in order to work out moral perfection, not only for ourselves, but for all mankind.

We believe that this principle and no other governs the continuous selection of the fittest of the peoples, and we are thinking of those who have actually contributed their part to the advance of human progress by placing upon the world the impress of their own national idea. History teaches us that this has often happened without the possession of an exceptionally powerful political empire....

GERMANY'S ROLE IN THE WORLD

It is not necessary to claim for the German idea that it will exist like the Roman either as the mistress of the world or not at all, but it is right to say that it will exist only as the co-mistress of the culture of the world, or it will not exist at all. The Anglo-Saxons have spread over such vast expanses that they seem to be on the point of assuming the cultural control of the world, thanks to their large numbers, their resources and their inborn strength. Russia, which is the largest and most populous non-Anglo-Saxon political entity, is bereft of its former world-embracing political prospects because of its inner lack of culture and its dissensions. France, the rival of England on either side of the ocean in the 18th century, and its superior in its general influence on the culture of the world, has voluntarily withdrawn from the competition of the world powers owing to the moral decline of her people who have condemned themselves to a numerically insufficient progeny. The German nation is the only one which has sufficiently developed by the side of the Anglo-Saxons, and is, moreover, numerically and inherently strong enough to claim for its national idea the right to participate in the shaping of the world which is to be.

The correct interpretation of this proposition implies that we shall be able to maintain our power only if we continue to spread the German idea. We may not cease nor stop, nor even grant a temporary restriction of our sphere of influence, for we have only these alternatives, either to sink back to the level of one of the territorial people, or to fight for a place by the side of the Anglo-Saxons. We are like the tree rooted in the cleft rock. We may press the rock asunder and grow, or the resistance is so great that we are stunted for lack of food....

THE CHOSEN PEOPLE

Remember, the German people are the chosen of God. On me the German Emperor, the spirit of God has descended. I am His sword, His weapon, and His vice-regent....Germany must have her place in the sun.

Kaiser Wilhelm II
To his soldiers on August 4, 1914.

GERMANY'S FATE IS ENGLAND

The German idea, therefore, can only live and increase, if its material foundations, viz., the number of Germans, the prosperity of Germany and the number and size of our world-interests continue to increase. As these foundations continue to grow they compel the Anglo-Saxons to make their decision between the following two propositions: Will they reconcile themselves to seeing our interests in the world maintain themselves by the side of their own, and come to an agreement with us concerning them? Or will they fight, with force of arms, to remain the sole mistress of the world? If they choose the first proposition, they do so because of our strength. If they choose the latter, it will depend on our strength whether we conquer, or surrender, or hold our own.

Germany's fate is England. The man who has studied the progress of the world during the last hundred years, and who knows something of the world today from his own observation, knows that there is only one important national-political question: ''Is the Anglo-Saxon type destined to gain the sole dominion in those parts of the world where things are still in the process of development, or will there be sufficient scope also for the German idea to take part in the shaping of the culture of the world on both sides of the ocean...?''

Exercise 1

Examining Cultural Universals

Instructions

When people are exposed through travel or education to foreign people and customs, the latter frequently seem absurd, outlandish, and sometimes inferior. This human tendency to feel superior about one's native values and customs is called ethnocentrism and occurs largely because people see others through the eyes of their own frame of reference or life experience. By exposing people to the customs of others, education has attempted to promote understanding, appreciation, and toleration of the world's cultural diversity.

While this task is vital, increased efforts should be made to emphasize the essential similarities of the human condition. People must become more aware of their common needs and desires. Only then will nations have the insight to unite in global efforts that deal with serious world problems. Starvation, malnutrition, poverty, disease, pollution, violence, and hatred respect no national boundaries or racial groups. In spite of racial, national, religious, and cultural differences, the essential similarities of people throughout the world are more important realities.

In order to deal realistically with human problems, nations must cooperate more and people must understand their common needs. Only then can a global psychology of cooperation and constructive, peaceful, problem-solving activities begin to predominate over warfare and violence. By completing the following activity, you can test your awareness of human similarities.

STEP 1. The class should break up into groups of four to six students.

STEP 2. Each small group should pretend they are on a commercial flight to Brazil. The pilot announces that you are passing over a city in Brazil, hidden from view by the clouds below. Even though you know nothing about the people of this city and their customs, discuss the following questions.

   a. What do the people of your city have in common with the people in the Brazilian city described above? (Make a list of all the similarities your group can identify. One student should be selected to record your list.)

   b. On what basis did you prepare your list?

STEP 3. After completing step two, the entire class should discuss and compare the lists prepared by the small groups.

Chapter **2**

Nationalism

Twentieth Century Nationalism:
The Roots of Conflict ?

INTRODUCTION

Rampant nationalism has cursed the twentieth century with a long series of conflicts great and small, foreign and domestic. World Wars I and II, more than a score of civil wars and several instances of limited big power interventionism, all can be traced to conflicting nationalistic aspirations. Even the unsuccessful popular revolution in Hungary (1956) and the ill-fated movement for constitutional reform in Czechoslovakia (1968) have exposed as myth the belief in a cooperative and dedicated supranational communist movement.

The following readings are meant to illustrate the variety and nature of twentieth century nationalism. In each case, ethnic, religious and racial differences have served as the convenient banners under which the adversaries could rally. In the Balkans, the struggle involved Slav and Teuton, in Israel, Moslem and Jew and in South Africa, Blacks and Whites. Yet each of these seemingly unrelated conflicts have originated from fundamental differences in the historical and cultural traditions of the groups involved. And to the misfortune of the combatants and innocents concerned, each derives its sustenance from hatred and strife.

The Annexation of Bosina-Herzegovina

Emperor Francis Joseph

The nationalistic aspirations of Slavic Serbia
were one of the underlying causes of World War
I. A sovereign nation since 1804, Serbia long
entertained the notion of territorial expansion in
the Balkan Peninsula of Europe. Her ultimate
goal was a pan-Serbian state which might also
include other Slavic speaking peoples of the
Balkans. Austria-Hungary, however, conspired
to thwart Serbia's ambitions. The presence of
twenty-three million disenfrancised Slavs in
her own Empire was largely responsible for
Austria-Hungary's policy of containment; a
large and powerful Serbia would only breed
discontent and possible revolution among the
hapless Slavs of Austria-Hungary.

25

In 1908, the Dual Monarchy sought to prevent further threats from Serbian nationalists by annexing Bosnia-Herzegovina, a Balkan state it had occupied since 1878. Serbia, believing Bosnia-Herzegovina and its large Serbian population to be her natural preserve, was thoroughly infuriated by the annexation. In the face of a militarily more powerful foe, her response was a carefully coordinated policy of subversion aimed at politically weakening Austria-Hungary. The proliferation of secret societies sponsoring sabotage, assassinations and revolutionary activity among "captive" Slavs were to serve that policy.

On June 28, 1914, Archduke Francis Ferdinand, the heir to the Austro-Hungarian throne, was murdered by a member of the Serbian Black Hand Society. Using the assassination as a pretext for war and hoping to finally eliminate the Serbian menace, Austria-Hungary declared war on Serbia. The declaration proved the immediate cause of World War I as a system of entangling alliances among the major powers of Europe turned what might have remained a localized affair into a continental conflict.

The following reading is Emperor Francis Joseph's decree announcing the annexation of Bosnia-Herzegovina.

Consider the following questions while reading:

1. What justification is given for the annexation of Bosnia-Herzegovina?
2. How will this annexation benefit Bosnia-Herzegovina?

J.H. Robinson and Charles Beard, editors, **Readings in Modern European History, Vol. II** (Lexington, Mass.: Ginn & Company, 1909), pp. 171-74.

AUSTRIA BROUGHT ORDER AND SECURITY

We, Francis Joseph, Emperor of Austria, King of Bohemia, and Apostolic King of Hungary, to the inhabitants of Bosnia and Herzegovina:

When a generation ago our troops crossed the borders of your lands, you were assured that they came not as foes, but as friends, with the firm determination to remedy the evils from which your fatherland had suffered so grievously for many years. This promise given at a serious moment has been honestly kept. It has been the constant endeavor of our government to guide the country by patient and systematic activity to a happier future.

To our great joy we can say that the seed then scattered in the furrows of a troubled soil has richly thrived. You yourselves must feel it a boon that order and security have replaced violence and oppression, that trade and traffic are constantly extending, that the elevating influence of education has been brought to bear in your country, and that under the shield of an orderly administration every man may enjoy the fruits of his labors.

It is the duty of us all to advance steadily along this path. With this goal before our eyes, we deem the moment come to give the inhabitants of the two lands a new proof of our trust in their political maturity. In order to raise Bosnia and Herzegovina to a higher level of political life we have resolved to grant both of those lands constitutional governments that are suited to the prevailing conditions and general interests, so as to create a legal basis for the representation of their wishes and needs. You shall henceforth have a voice when decisions are made

EXTENDING OUR POWER

...we extend our suzerainty over Bosnia and Herzegovina, and it is our will that the order of succession of our House be extended to these lands also.

concerning your domestic affairs, which, as hitherto, will have a separate administration. But the necessary premise for the introduction of this provincial constitution is the creation of a clear and unambiguous legal status for the two lands.

A NEW ORDER

For this reason, and also remembering the ties that existed of yore between our glorious ancestors on the Hungarian throne and these lands, we extend our suzerainty [rule] over Bosnia and Herzegovina, and it is our will that the order of succession of our House be extended to these lands also. The inhabitants of the two lands thus share all the benefits which a lasting confirmation of the present relation can offer. The new order of things will be a guarantee that civilization and prosperity will find a sure footing in your home.

Archduke Francis Ferdinand and his wife Sophie, minutes before the assassination. United Press International, Inc.

Inhabitants of Bosnia and Herzegovina:

Among the many cares of our throne, solicitude for your material and spiritual welfare shall not be the last. The exalted idea of equal rights for all before the law, a share in the legislation and administration of the provincial affairs, equal protection for all religious creeds, languages, and racial differences, all these high possessions you shall enjoy in full measure. The freedom of the individual and the welfare of the whole will be the aim of our government in the two lands. You will surely show yourselves worthy of the trust placed in you, by attachment and loyalty to us and to our House. And thus we hope that the noble harmony between the prince and the people, that dearest pledge of all social progress, will ever accompany us on our common path.

Arrest of assassin Gavrillo Princip, whose fatal bullet sparked World War I.

Serbia's Reply To Annexation

The Narodna Odbrana

The founding of the *Narodna Odbrana* (Society of National Defense) was one of the responses of Serbian nationalists to the annexation of Bosnia-Herzegovina. The following is the program of the Society in which its rationale, goals and methods are declared.

Consider the following questions while reading:

1. How are the actions of Austria described?
2. What is the new concept of nationalism?
3. What is the purpose of the *Narodna Odbrana*?

From **Europe In The Nineteenth Century 1815-1914** edited by Eugene N. Anderson, Stanley J. Pincetl, Jr. and Donald J. Zeigler, copyright © 1961 by The Bobs-Merrill Company, Inc. This reading is taken from pages 304-06, 333-35.

AUSTRIA'S PROVOCATION

The *Narodna Odbrana* maintains that the annexation of Bosnia and Herzegovina is clearly an invasion of our country from the north; thus it regards Austria as our principal and greatest enemy and so represents it to our people. The exposition of this idea is in no way fanaticism or chauvinism but a healthy and entirely understandable task, an elementary duty, a need exactly like that to impress the fact that two times two makes four.

The Serbs have never hated for the mere sake of hating, but they have always loved freedom and independence. We have already said in another place that, just as once the Turks from the south pressed upon us, now the Austrians from the north are coming. If the *Narodna Odbrana* is preaching the need for a struggle with Austria, it is but proclaiming the sacred truth which arises out of our national position. If hate and fanaticism develop, they are but natural phenomena which come as results and not as an end. For us the goal is our existence, our freedom. If hate against Austria breaks out, we are not the ones who have sown it; Austria is the sower of the hate, through her action against us which forces us to struggle until she is destroyed.

A NEW CONCEPT OF NATIONALISM

Today everywhere a new concept of nationalism has become prevalent. Nationalism (the feeling of nationality) is no longer a historical or poetical feeling, but the true practical expression of life. Among the French, Germans, and English, and among all other civilized peoples, nationalism has grown into something quite new; in it lies the concept of bread, space, air, commerce, competition in everything. Only among us is it still in the old form; that is, it is the fruit of spiritual suffering rather than of reasonable understanding and national advantage. If we speak of freedom and union, we parade far too much the phrases ''breaking our chains'' and ''freeing the slaves''; we call far too much upon our former Serbian glory and think too little of the fact that the freeing of subjected areas and their union with Serbia are necessary to our citizens, our merchants, and our peasants on the grounds of the most elementary needs of culture and trade, of food and space. If one were to explain to our sharp-eyed people our national task as one closely connected with the needs of everyday life, our people would take up the work in a greater spirit of sacrifice than is today the case. We must tell our people that the freedom of Bosnia is necessary, not just because of their feeling of sympathy with their brothers who suffer there, but also because of commerce and its connection with the sea; national union is necessary because of the stronger development of a common culture....

The Balkans States of Europe on the eve of World War I.

OUR NATIONAL IDEAL

Article 1. This organisation has been created with the object of realising the national ideal: The union of all the Serbs. All Serbs...and all who are sincerely devoted to this cause, may become members....

Article 3. This organisation bears the name "Union or Death...."

Article 4. To accomplish its task, the organisation...organises revolutionary action in all territories inhabited by Serbs.

Statutes of the Pan-Serbian Black Hand Society (1911)

Along with the task of explaining to our people the danger threatening us from Austria, the *Narodna Odbrana* has also the other important tasks of explaining to them, while preserving our holy national memories, this new, healthy, fruitful conception of nationalism, and of convincing them to work for national freedom and unity....

AUSTRIA MUST PAY!

The change which took place in Serbia after the annexation is in great part due to the efforts of the *Narodna Odbrana*. As a true national defender, our organization will endure to the end; and if the end comes, if a situation obtains like that at the time of the annexation, thanks to its present activity the *Narodna Odbrana* will face the task which it will have to fulfill then with a tenfold greater ability than it had at the time of the annexation. Through its present activity it is preparing itself and the country for the real function for which it has come into being.

All in all, the *Narodna Odbrana* aims through its work to advance upon the enemy on the day of reckoning with a sound, nationally conscious, and internally reconciled Serbian people, a nation of Sokols, rifle clubs, heroes — in fact, the fear and terror of the enemy — reliant front-rank fighters and executors of Serbia's holy cause.

If this succeeds, all will be well for us; woe to us if we fail.

Viewpoint  7

Palestine: The Jewish Homeland

Theodor Herzl

Theodor Herzl (1860-1904), an Austro-Hungarian Jewish leader, is considered the father of modern Zionism (an international movement for advancing the state of Israel). In the summer of 1895, he wrote his momentous *Der Judenstaat* (*The Jewish State*) in which he historically evaluated the ''Jewish Question'' and pleaded the case for a Jewish Homeland. In August, 1897, Herzl was influential in convening the first Zionist Congress in Basel where it was declared that Palestine would be the homeland of the Jews. Acknowledging his preeminent role in the Zionist movement, Herzl prophetically said that ''at Basel I founded the Jewish State. If I said this out loud today, I would be greeted by universal laughter. In five years perhaps, and certainly in fifty years, everyone will perceive it.'' Fifty years later, in 1948, the State of Israel was proclaimed by the Jews in Palestine and accorded *de facto* recognition by the United States.

Consider the following questions while reading:

1. How does Herzl explain Anti-Semitism?
2. What is the grave situation of the Jews?
3. How is the plan for a new Jewish state justified and described?

Theodor Herzl, **The Jewish State** (London: H. Pordes, 1967), pp. 7, 14-16, 22-24, 27-30.
Reprinted with permission.

THE HISTORIC "JEWISH QUESTION"

The idea which I have developed in this pamphlet is a very old one: it is the restoration of the Jewish State....

The Jewish question still exists. It would be foolish to deny it. It is a remnant of the Middle Ages, which civilised nations do not even yet seem able to shake off, try as they will. They certainly showed a generous desire to do so when they emancipated us. The Jewish question exists wherever Jews live in perceptible numbers. Where it does not exist, it is carried by Jews in the course of their migrations. We naturally move to those places where we are not persecuted, and there our presence produces persecution. This is the case in every country, and will remain so, even in those highly civilised — for instance, France — till the Jewish question finds a solution on a political basis. The unfortunate Jews are now carrying Anti-Semitism into England; they have already introduced it into America.

AGE OLD ANTI-SEMITISM

I believe that I understand Anti-Semitism, which is really a highly complex movement. I consider it from a Jewish standpoint, yet without fear or hatred. I believe that I can see what elements there are in it of vulgar sport, of common trade jealousy, of inherited prejudice, of religious intolerance, and also of pretended self-defence. I think the Jewish question is no more a social than a religious one, notwithstanding that it sometimes takes these and other forms. It is a national question, which can only be solved by making it a political world-question to be discussed and settled by the civilised nations of the world in council.

We are a people — one people.

We have honestly endeavoured everywhere to merge ourselves in the social life of surrounding communities and to preserve only the faith of our fathers. We are not permitted to do so. In vain are we loyal patriots, our loyalty in some places running to extremes; in vain do we make the same sacrifices of life and property as our fellow-citizens; in vain do we strive to increase the fame of our native land in science and art, or her wealth by trade and commerce. In countries where we have lived for centuries we are still cried down as strangers, and often by those whose ancestors were not yet domiciled in the land where Jews had already made experience of suffering....If we could only be left in peace.

But I think we shall not be left in peace.

Oppression and persecution cannot exterminate us. No nation on earth has survived such struggles and sufferings as we have gone through. Jew-baiting has merely stripped off our weaklings; the strong among us were invariably true to their race when persecution broke out against them....

Old prejudices against us still lie deep in the hearts of the people. He who would have proofs of this need only listen to the people where they speak with frankness and simplicity: proverb and fairy-tale are both Anti-Semitic. A nation is everywhere a great child, which can certainly be educated; but its education would, even in most favourable circumstances, occupy such a vast amount of time that we could, as already mentioned, remove our own difficulties by other means long before the process was accomplished....

THE GRAVE SITUATION OF THE JEWS

No one can deny the gravity of the situation of the Jews. Wherever they live in perceptible numbers, they are more or less persecuted. Their equality before the law, granted by statute, has become practically a dead letter. They are debarred from filling even moderately high positions, either in the army, or in any public or private capacity. And attempts are made to thrust them out of business also: ''Don't buy of Jews!''

Attacks in Parliaments, in assemblies, in the Press, in the pulpit, in the streets, on journeys — for example, their exclusion from certain hotels — even in places of recreation, become daily more numerous: the form of persecution varying according to the countries and social circles in which they occur. In Russia, impositions are levied on Jewish villages; in Roumania, a few persons are put to death; in Germany, they get a good beating occasionally; in Austria, Anti-Semites exercise terrorism over all public life; in Algeria, there are travelling agitators; in Paris, the Jews are shut out of the so-called best social circles and excluded from clubs. Shades of anti-Jewish feeling are innumerable. But this is not to be an attempt to make out a doleful category of Jewish hardships; it is futile to linger over details, however painful they may be....

We are one people — our enemies have made us one in our despite, as repeatedly happens in history. Distress binds us together, and, thus united, we suddenly discover our strength. Yes, we are strong enough to form a State, and, indeed, a model State. We possess all human and material resources necessary for the purpose....

THE SOCIETY OF JEWS

Let the sovereignty be granted us over a portion of the globe large enough to satisfy the rightful requirements of a nation; the rest we shall manage for ourselves.

A JEWISH HOMELAND

"His Majesty's Government view with favour the establishment in Palestine of a national home for the Jewish people, and will use their best endeavours to facilitate the achievement of this object, it being clearly understood that nothing shall be done which may prejudice the civil and religious rights of existing non-Jewish communities in Palestine, or the rights and political status enjoyed by Jews in any other country."

A letter from Lord Balfour, former British Prime Minister sent on November, 2, 1917, to Lord Rothschild, a leading British Zionist.

The creation of a new State is neither ridiculous nor impossible. We have in our day witnessed the process in connection with nations which were not in the bulk of the middle class, but poorer, less educated, and consequently weaker than ourselves. The Governments of all countries scourged by Anti-Semitism will be keenly interested in assisting us to obtain the sovereignty we want.

The plan, simple in design, but complicated in execution, will be carried out by two agencies: The Society of Jews and the Jewish Company.

The Society of Jews will do the preparatory work in the domains of science and politics, which the Jewish Company will afterwards practically apply.

The Jewish Company will see to the realisation of the business interests of departing Jews, and will organise commerce and trade in the new country....

PALESTINE: THE JEWISH HOMELAND

Those Jews who fall in with our idea of a State will attach themselves to the Society, which will thereby be authorised to confer and treat with Governments in the name of our people. The Society will thus be acknowledged in its relations with Governments as a State-creating power. This acknowledgment will practically create the State.

The roots of genocide: Polish Jews rounded up by Nazi storm troopers, 1939. United Press International, Inc.

Should the Powers declare themselves willing to admit our sovereignty over a neutral piece of land, then the Society will enter into negotiations for the possession of this land. Here two territories come under consideration, Palestine and Argentina. In both countries important experiments in colonisation have been made, though on the mistaken principle of a gradual infiltration of Jews. An infiltration is bound to end badly. It continues till the inevitable moment when the native population feels itself threatened, and forces the Government to stop a further influx of Jews. Immigration is consequently futile unless based on an assured supremacy.

The Society of Jews will treat with the present masters of the land, putting itself under the protectorate of the European Powers, if they prove friendly to the plan. We could offer the present possessors of the land enormous advantages, take upon ourselves part of the public debt, build new roads for traffic, which our presence in the country would render necessary, and do many other things. The creation of our State would be beneficial to adjacent countries, because the cultivation of a strip of land increases the value of its surrounding districts in innumerable ways....

Shall we choose Palestine or Argentina...?

Palestine is our ever-memorable historic home. The very name of Palestine would attract our people with a force of marvellous potency....We should there form a portion of the rampart of Europe against Asia, an outpost of civilisation as opposed to barbarism. We should as a neutral State remain in contact with all Europe, which would have to guarantee our existence. The sanctuaries of Christendom would be safeguarded by assigning to them an extra-territorial status such as is well known to the law of nations. We should form a guard of honour about these sanctuaries, answering for the fulfillment of this duty with our existence. This guard of honour would be the great symbol of the solution of the Jewish Question after eighteen centuries of Jewish suffering....

Viewpoint  8

Palestine:
The Arab Homeland

First Arab Students' Congress

Since its inception in 1948, the history of the
state of Israel has been one of episodic warfare
between Arabs and Jews. The Zionist argument
of ancient historic rights to the land is rejected
by the Arabs who often claim a more ancient
heritage. The problem has been exacerbated by
the displacement of several million homeless
Palestinian refugees and by the involvement of
the major world powers. Anticipating the contemporary Middle Eastern dilemma, many
Arab groups began espousing Arab nationalism
prior to 1948 and depicting Zionists as the
enemies of the Arab peoples. In December,
1938, a group of Arab students met in Brussels,
Belgium and drafted the following manifesto.

Consider the following questions while reading:

1. How is an Arab defined?
2. What is the new Arab renaissance?
3. Why are Jews considered a problem?

Sylvia G. Haim, editor, **Arab Nationalism** (Berkeley: University of California Press, 1962), pp.
100-02. Copyright © 1962 by The Regents of the University of California; reprinted by permission of the University of California Press.

OUR NATIONAL PACT

I am an Arab, and I believe that the Arabs constitute one nation. The sacred right of this nation is to be sovereign in her own affairs. Her ardent nationalism drives her to liberate the Arab homeland, to unite all its parts, and to found political, economic, and social institutions more sound and more compatible than the existing ones. The aim of this nationalism is to raise up the standard of living and to increase the material and the spiritual good of the people; it also aspires to share in working for the good of the human collectivity; it strives to realize this by continuous work based on national organization.

I pledge myself to God, that I will strive in this path to my utmost, putting the national interest above any other consideration.

WHO ARE THE ARABS?

The Arabs: All who are Arab in their language, culture, and loyalty [defined in a footnote as "national feeling"], those are the Arabs. The Arab is the individual who belongs to the nation made up of those people.

The Arab Homeland: It is the land which has been, or is, inhabited by an Arab majority, in the above sense, in Asia and Africa. As such it is a whole which cannot be divided or partitioned. It is a sacred heritage no inch of which may be trifled with. Any compromise in this respect is invalid and is national treason.

Arab Nationalism: It is the feeling for the necessity of independence and unity which the inhabitants of the Arab lands share [a footnote adds: "The Arab emigrants abroad are included in this definition."]. It is based on the unity of the homeland, of language, culture, history, and a sense of the common good.

The Arab Movement: It is the new Arab renaissance which pervades the Arab nation. Its motive force is her glorious past, her remarkable vitality and the awareness of her present and future interests. This movement strives continuously and in an organized manner toward well-defined aims. These aims are to liberate and unite the Arab homeland, to found political, economic, and social organizations more sound than the existing ones, and to attempt afterward to work for the good of the human collectivity and its progress. These aims are to be realized by definite means drawn from the preparedness of the Arabs and their particular situation, as well as from the experience of the West. They will be realized without subscribing to any particular creed of the modern Western ones such as Fascism, Communism, or Democracy.

ARABS PRECEDED JEWS

The argument of the Jews with respect to their rights in Palestine, which is based on their immigration into it two thousand years ago, is "an argument not worthy of consideration or attention," as is textually recorded in the report of the King Crane Commission which came to Palestine in 1919 to ascertain the wishes of the population in Syria and Lebanon. And this argument, supposing that it were valid, is rather in favor of the Arabs than of the Jews, because the Arabs preceded the Jews in Palestine. Robinson, in his book THE HISTORY OF ISRAEL, has written about the Arabs of Palestine. "They migrated into Palestine three thousand years before the birth of Christ, coming from the Arabian Peninsula; in spite of this their features and their looks are still apparent in the physiognomy of their descendants." Add to this the fact that the Arab element in Palestine was able in some regions to preserve its independence continuously, even during the golden age of the Jews, so that when the Jewish conquerors were gradually evacuated from Palestine the region came within the zone of influence of the Arab states, until finally it became purely Arab after the great Arab upsurge through Islam.

Muhammad Jamil Baihum
"Arabism and Jewry in Syria"

The Arab National Idea: It is a national idea which proscribes the existence of racial, regional, and communal fanaticisms. It respects the freedom of religious observance, and individual freedoms such as the freedom of opinion, work, and assembly, unless they conflict with the public good. The Arab national idea cannot be contradictory to the good of real racial and religious minorities; it aims rather at treating all sincere patriots on the principle of equality of rights and duties.

FOREIGNERS IN OUR LAND
We have said that the Arab countries belong to the Arabs and that benefits therefrom must accrue to them. By Arabs we mean those whom the political report has included under this appellation. As for those elements who are not Arabized and who do not intend to be Arabized but are, rather, intent on putting obstacles in the way of the Arab nation, they are foreign to the Arab nation. The most prominent problem of this kind is that of the Jews in Palestine.

Children play amidst squalor of Arab refugee camp in Jordan, 1969. **Wide World Photos**

43

If we looked at the Jews in Palestine from an economic angle we would find that their economy is totally incompatible with the Arab economy. The Jews are attempting to build up a Jewish state in Palestine and to bring into this state great numbers of their kind from all over the world. Palestine is a small country, and they will therefore have to industrialize it so that this large number of inhabitants can find subsistence. And in order to make their industry a success they will have to find markets for their products. For this they depend on the Arab market; their products will therefore flood the Arab countries and compete with Arab industries. This is very harmful to the Arabs.

Moreover, Palestine, placed as it is between the Arab countries in Asia and Africa, occupies an important position in land, sea, and air communications. A foreign state in Palestine will impede these communications and have a harmful effect on commerce. And even if the Jews in Palestine presented no danger other than the economic, this would be enough for us to oppose them and to put an end to their intrigues, so that we may ensure for our country a happy and glorious future.

Viewpoint

South Africa:
The Case for the White Afrikaners

Roeloef F. Botha

The apartheid policy of the government of
South Africa has received world-wide con-
demnation. The white minority government has
been accused of callous racism for its efforts to
exclude the black majority in South Africa from
active participation in that nation's political
processes. However supporters of apartheid
claim that the government's policy is nationalistic, not racial. The South African whites
(called Africaners), it is argued, have inhabited
the country for over 300 years and majority rule
would probably deny them virtually all rights in
their homeland. The following reading is by
Roelof F. Botha, the Foreign Minister of South
Africa. It offers a brief historical and contemporary overview of the South African
''problem'' and attempts both to explain and
justify the official Afrikaner position.

Consider the following questions while reading:

1. List several of Botha's arguments which explain why South
   Africa has a right to exist as a white African nation.
2. List some of the strengths and weaknesses of Botha's arguments. What are the reasons for your choices?

Roelof F. Botha, ''Why South Africa Has Right to Exist As a White African Nation,'' **Intellect**,
August 1977, pp. 35-36. Reprinted with permission.

THE SOUTH AFRICAN SCENE

The South African Scene is observed from many angles abroad and from differing points of view. In general, a majority of commentators proceed from the same assumption — the policy of the South African government is wrong. It is, of course, relatively easy to condemn a policy as unjust without offering an alternative which is more just.

Take, for instance, the fashionable concept of majority rule, which is proffered by many as a miraculous cure for all the ills of my country. In how many of the countries of the world does one find majority rule in the sense in which Americans understand that concept? Most Americans may agree that one of the most important principles of morality is the application of its norms and demands on an equal basis to all. Morality, by its very nature, can not be selective. How many who demand majority rule for South Africa in the context of American democracy are willing to guarantee to South Africans similar rights? I say, if you can not give the guarantee, do not make the demand.

I do not deny the existence of problems in South Africa or dispute the need for change in my country, but I do say that much of the information on my country is completely unsubstantiated, unbelievably one-sided and distorted, and lacking in perspective. The picture which more than often emerges of South Africa in the outside world, and also in the U.S., is one of unmitigated racism and inhumanity against black South Africans. The impression is being created that everything the South African government does is inherently evil, that the South African government degrades the black man, that the black South African has no political rights, and that the object of the South African government is the perpetual entrenchment of white superiority. This is just not so.

HISTORICAL PERSPECTIVE

Let me briefly give some historical perspective to indicate the dimensions of our situation.

The South African policy of multinational development goes back 300 years to the arrival of the first white settlers. Throughout the two centuries which followed the convergence on South Africa of the white people by sea and the blacks overland from the areas to the north, the over-all tendency was not only for the whites, but also the various black peoples, to settle in distinct parts of the country. It was during this time that the framework for the homelands policy came into being naturally and historically as each area evolved its own institutions of government, systems of land tenure, traditions, cultures, languages, and economies. In South Africa, the disparities among a heterogenous black population which existed 300 years ago did not come about as a result of Prime Minister Vorster's policies.

The divisions in South African society are of a natural and historical origin of sociological affinity. The choice lay between the relative merits of recognizing the existing political, geographic, and cultural divisions, or attempting to eliminate them and force all the various societies into one artificial unity. The tragic experiences of other parts of the world in attempting to enforce the unity of diversities encourage little optimism in South Africa that the attempt would have any greater chances of success there. A more likely result would be the transfer of political power from one group to another, rather than the radical redistribution of power which critics of South Africa suggest will satisfy their basic criterion of significant change.

A development with profound implications for the international political order was the emergence of a deeply felt African nationalism. It must, however, not be forgotten that, over a period of 300 years of constant struggle towards untrammeled independence, the whites of South Africa have evolved their own nationalism, which they will not abdicate. Any just solution must therefore accommodate both black and white nationalisms. Attempts by either nationalism to dominate or overthrow the other will be resisted and could, if alternatives are not found, lead to a conflict with awesome consequences, not only for black and white in South Africa, but further afield.... This the South African government wishes to avoid. Its detractors are, in fact, wittingly or unwittingly inviting such a struggle — and, thus, courting disaster.

JUDGING SOUTH AFRICA'S POLICIES

Important changes have been introduced in South Africa to improve relations between black and white. More will be introduced. The significance of these changes are seldom correctly assessed. Indeed, they are often rejected by our critics on the grounds that they have no direct bearing on the political power structure. This is precisely where the greatest misunderstanding arises. Critics of the South African government refuse to admit that a just political dispensation can be achieved in South Africa by a division of political power which can accommodate black and white nationalisms, while, at the same time, introducing far-reaching or significant changes in discriminatory measures based on color.

In expressing judgment on the implementation of South Africa's policy it also is important to know that:

• Hundreds of thousands of black workers from other countries of Africa voluntarily come to South Africa for employment, many of them entering the country illegally for that purpose. The average industrial wages for blacks in South Africa are 80% higher than in Ghana, which has one of the highest wage structures in Africa.

• The per capita income of Johannesburg blacks more than doubled between 1970 and 1975. In the same period, white per capita income increased by 58%.

• The consumer market of Johannesburg blacks was worth $750,000,000 in 1975. This compares with independent Botswana's Gross National Product of $175,000,000 in 1973 with a population of about half that of the blacks of Johannesburg.

• The income of black family units in Johannesburg increased from about $1,200 in 1970 to about $2,620 in 1975. The equivalent in purchasing power in the U.S. would be roughly two-and-a-half times these amounts.

• Hundreds of millions of dollars are spent in South Africa to provide free or virtually free medical services to blacks....

• The combined rate of population growth of the black peoples of South Africa is 3.23% — the highest in Africa.

• More than 21% of the total black population of South Africa is attending school, which amounts to more than 4,000,000 pupils. This compares favorably not only with the figures of 10% for the rest of Africa, but also with those for many European and other countries. Of even greater significance is the phenomenal increase in black school attendance at the secondary level....

In contrast to the lack of press freedom in many countries of the world, a large and influential section of the press vigorously criticizes the policies of the South African government daily. Opposition is not limited to the press and is frequently expressed by black leaders in South Africa. No action is or can be taken under South African law against opponents and critics as long as their opposition is conducted in a constitutional manner....

White South Africans did not conquer black nations and did not steal their land. The areas occupied by the White Trekkers (pioneers) to the north were for the most part completely uninhabited due to what the blacks still call the ''mfekane'' or ''crushing.''

THE RIGHT TO EXIST

White South Africans are an African nation and insist on the right to exist and govern themselves. However, what is apparently demanded from them is that they should willingly accept their own demise in their own country because they wish to preserve that which is dear to them as a nation. Where is the morality in this type of demand? Where is the equality and justice in the clamor for censuring South Africa on account of alleged inequalities when the overwhelming majority of the peoples of the world know no freedom, no security of person, and never participate in any process to elect their governments? In contrast, South Africa's principal aim is to allow each nation, black and white, to achieve sovereign independence.

The problem in South Africa is basically not one of race, but of nationalism, which is a worldwide problem. There is a white nationalism and there are several black nationalisms. These are realities. A just and viable solution of the problems must cater to the aims of all these nationalisms.

NATIONALISM AND APARTHEID

At the root of the separate development program lies the nationalism...of the Afrikaner (White South African)...It is indeed an error to see apartheid as expressive only of an attitude of the white man toward the black. For nationalism as such is not a question of color feeling, and it is nationalism, rather racialism, that the honest inquirer has basically to comprehend.

Charles A. W. Manning, **Foreign Affairs**, October, 1964

South African Roelof F. Botha confers with Rhodesian Prime Minister Ian Smith.

Embassy of South Africa.

One of the black nations, Transkei, was established as a state, with full sovereignty, on Oct. 26, 1976. That it has not been recognized as a full member of the family of nations derogates not at all from the physical fact that it is an African nation, formerly subject to white rule, now fully in command of its own destiny, having achieved its independence through peaceful, constitutional means. Withholding recognition of Transkei is based on the application of double standards. Transkei meets the criteria of statehood more convincingly than a few dozen states that are now members of the UN — *e.g.*, size of land area and population, per capita income, budget, educational advancement, economic base, and political system.

To conclude, the only choice we have before us in Southern Africa is either to continue on the sterile course of confrontation and recrimination or to make a sincere endeavor to come to an understanding with one another and to listen to the other man's point of view with an open mind. Communication or confrontation — that is our choice.

South Africa:
The Case for the Black Africans

Nelson Mandela

Nelson Mandela was a successful lawyer and
leader of the African National Congress, the
oldest nationalist group in Africa. In 1960, he
was sentenced by the apartheid South African
government to five years imprisonment for
incitement to strike and traveling without a
valid passport. In October, 1963, a group of
black nationalists, who were intimates of
Mandela, were arrested and charged with
sabotage and conspiracy to overthrow the
government by revolution. Mandela was taken
from prison and made to stand trial as one of the
accused. On April 20, 1964, he dramatically
opened the case for the defence with the
following speech.

Consider the following questions while reading:

1. Why is South Africa a land of extreme contrasts?
2. How does White Supremacy affect Africans?
3. What do Africans want?

Nelson Mandela, **No Easy Walk to Freedom** (London: Heinemann, 1965), pp. 162-64, 170,
184-89. Reprinted with permission.

A LAND OF EXTREME CONTRASTS

South Africa is the richest country in Africa, and could be one of the richest countries in the world. But it is a land of extremes and remarkable contrasts. The Whites enjoy what may well be the highest standard of living in the world, whilst Africans live in poverty and misery. Forty per cent of the Africans live in hopelessly overcrowded and, in some cases, drought-stricken Reserves, where soil erosion and the overworking of the soil makes it impossible for them to live properly off the land. Thirty per cent are labourers, labour tenants, and squatters on White farms and work and live under conditions similar to those of the serfs of the Middle Ages. The other 30 per cent live in towns where they have developed economic and social habits which bring them closer in many respects to White standards. Yet most Africans, even in this group, are impoverished by low incomes and high cost of living....

DISEASE RATE AND EDUCATIONAL STANDARDS

Poverty goes hand in hand with malnutrition and disease. The incidence of malnutrition and deficiency diseases is very high amongst Africans. Tuberculosis, pellagra, kwashiorkor, gastroenteritis, and scurvy bring death and destruction of health. The incidence of infant mortality is one of the highest in the world. According to the Medical Officer of Health for Pretoria, tuberculosis kills forty people a day (almost all Africans), and in 1961 there were 58,491 new cases reported. These diseases not only destroy the vital organs of the body, but they result in retarded mental conditions and lack of initiative, and reduce powers of concentration. The secondary results of such conditions affect the whole community and the standard of work performed by African labourers.

The complaint of Africans, however, is not only that they are poor and the Whites are rich, but that the laws which are made by the Whites are designed to preserve this situation. There are two ways to break out of poverty. The first is by formal education, and the second is by the worker acquiring a greater skill at his work and thus higher wages. As far as Africans are concerned, both these avenues of advancement are deliberately curtailed by legislation.

The present Government has always sought to hamper

Africans in their search for education. One of their early acts, after coming into power, was to stop subsidies for African school feeding. Many African children who attended schools depended on this supplement to their diet. This was a cruel act.

There is compulsory education for all White children at virtually no cost to their parents, be they rich or poor. Similar facilities are not provided for the African children, though there are some who receive such assistance. African children, however, generally have to pay more for their schooling than Whites....

The quality of education is also different. According to the Bantu Educational Journal, only 5,660 African children in the whole of South Africa passed their J.C. in 1962, and in that year only 362 passed matric. This is presumably consistent with the policy of Bantu education about which the present Prime Minister said, during the debate on the Bantu Education Bill in 1953:

When I have control of Native education I will reform it so that Natives will be taught from childhood to realize that equality with Europeans is not for them....People who believe in equality are not desirable teachers for Natives. When my Department controls Native education it will know for what class of higher education a Native is fitted, and whether he will have a chance in life to use his knowledge.

A RELIC OF THE PAST

It is not necessary for me to speak at length about South Africa. It is a museum piece in our time, a hangover from the dark past of mankind, a relic of an age which everywhere else is dead or dying. Here the cult of race superiority and of white supremacy is worshipped like a god....Thus it is that the golden age of Africa's independence is also the dark age of South Africa's decline and retrogression.

Albert John Luthuli, former Zulu chief of South Africa, upon receiving the 1960 Nobel Peace Prize.

WHITE SUPREMACY AND OPPRESSION

The lack of human dignity experienced by Africans is the direct result of the policy of White supremacy. White supremacy implies Black inferiority. Legislation designed to preserve White supremacy entrenches this notion. Menial tasks in South Africa are invariably performed by Africans. When anything has to be carried or cleaned the White man will look around for an African to do it for him, whether the African is employed by him or not. Because of this sort of attitude, Whites tend to

Two students carry the body of a friend killed by police during a 1976 riot in Soweto, South Africa.   Wide World Photos

55

regard Africans as a separate breed. They do not look upon them as people with families of their own; they do not realize that they have emotions — that they fall in love like White people do; that they want to be with their wives and children like White people want to be with theirs; that they want to earn enough money to support their families properly, to feed and clothe them and send them to school. And what 'house-boy'' or 'garden-boy' or labourer can ever hope to do this?

Pass laws, which to the Africans are among the most hated bits of legislation in South Africa, render any African liable to police surveillance at any time. I doubt whether there is a single African male in South Africa who has not at some stage had a brush with the police over his pass. Hundreds and thousands of Africans are thrown into jail each year under pass laws. Even worse than this is the fact that pass laws keep husband and wife apart and lead to the breakdown of family life....

"I AM PREPARED TO DIE"

Africans want to be paid a living wage. Africans want to perform work which they are capable of doing, and not work which the Government declares them to be capable of. Africans want to be allowed to live where they obtain work, and not be endorsed out of an area because they were not born there. Africans want to be allowed to own land in places where they work, and not to be obliged to live in rented houses which they can never call their own. Africans want to be part of the general population, and not confined to living in their own ghettoes. African men want to have their wives and children to live with them where they work, and not be forced into an unnatural existence in men's hostels. African women want to be with their menfolk and not be left permanently widowed in the Reserves. Africans want to be allowed out after eleven o'clock at night and not to be confined to their rooms like little children. Africans want to be allowed to travel in their own country and to seek work where they want to and not where the Labour Bureau tells them to. Africans want a just share in the whole of South Africa; they want security and a stake in society.

Above all, we want equal political rights, because without them our disabilities will be permanent. I know this sounds revolutionary to the Whites in this country, because the majority of voters will be Africans. This makes the White man fear democracy.

But this fear cannot be allowed to stand in the way of the only solution which will guarantee racial harmony and freedom for all. It is not true that the enfranchisement of all will result in racial domination. Political division, based on colour, is entirely artificial and, when it disappears, so will the domination of one colour group by another. The ANC* has spent half a century fighting against racialism. When it triumphs it will not change that policy.

This then is what the ANC is fighting. Their struggle is a truly national one. It is a struggle of the African people, inspired by their own suffering and their own experience. It is a struggle for the right to live.

During my lifetime I have dedicated myself to this struggle of the African people. I have fought against White domination, and I have fought against Black domination. I have cherished the ideal of a democratic and free society in which all persons live together in harmony and with equal opportunities. It is an ideal which I hope to live for and to achieve. But if needs be, it is an ideal for which I am prepared to die.

*ANC — African National Congress, founded in 1912 to defend the rights of the Black Africans.

2

Understanding Nationalism

Instructions

An appreciation and understanding of national ideals and achievements should be promoted and respected by all citizens. But an extreme and irrational patriotism represents a key feature of the racist and fascist mentality. The statement "My country right or wrong" expresses well the spirit of this unreasoned nationalism. It was originally made by Stephen Decatur, an American naval hero in the War of 1812. The Nazis placed his slogan over the entrance to the Buchenwald death camp in Germany. People cannot morally condone unethical actions and violence simply because they advance the wealth, power, and selfish interests of their country. In order to promote more international cooperation and understanding, it will be necessary for nations to overcome their feelings of suspicion and extreme nationalism.

Examine the following statements and try to identify attitudes that express a cooperative and worldminded outlook. Mark (N) for any statements expressing very nationalistic or selfish global views. Mark (W) for any statements expressing world-minded and cooperative global views. Mark (O) for any statements that express neither nationalistic nor worldminded ideas.

> N = Nationalistic
> W = Worldminded
> O = Neither

_____ 1. Our nation should be able to prevent certain racial and religious groups from entering and living here.

_____ 2. Immigrants who might compete with our own workers should not be allowed to come into our country.

_____ 3. Our nation is not morally superior to other countries.

_____ 4. An international charter giving all people equal rights would be a dangerous idea.

_____ 5. It would be a good idea to have an international trade committee set prices for all exported manufactured goods.

_____ 6. We should always be willing to fight for our country without questions about the motives for engaging in war.

_____ 7. A world government that guaranteed the welfare of all nations would help prevent war.

_____ 8. International trade agreements that promote world economic conditions at our nation's expense should be opposed.

_____ 9. One should think in terms of world citizenship rather than national citizenship.

_____ 10. Our nation should not cooperate in world disarmament programs because we can never trust the communists.

_____ 11. People should be allowed to live wherever they want to in the world.

_____ 12. No nations should participate in a world government that requires giving up any national rights or freedoms.

_____ 13. People should be willing to lower their standard of living to help other people in the world.

_____ 14. Teaching loyalty to our nation should be a primary goal of American education.

_____ 15. Only an international army or police force should be allowed to have armaments.

_____ 16. War is an unreasonable way to settle international disputes.

_____ 17. To promote peace, nations must be willing to give up some national independence to the authority of a world government.

_____ 18. It is essential that we consider our own U.S. citizens to be of more importance and value than those of other nations.

_____ 19. Because of our material prosperity and democratic government, people are happier in the United States than they are in other countries.

_____ 20. Loyalty to one's moral convictions is more important than loyalty to one's nation.

_____ 21. Foreign criticism of the U.S. is motivated primarily by envy of our economic and political achievements.

_____ 22. Those who are overly critical of the United States should be encouraged to leave the country.

_____ 23. Disarmament is dangerous to the U.S. because we live in a hostile world and must always maintain the most powerful military force.

_____ 24. We must join forces with all anti-communist nations.

_____ 25. Because of our moral and material superiority, the U.S. should have more voice in making United Nations policy than other countries.

___ 26. If it weren't for the communists, nations of the world could more easily find peaceful solutions to global problems.

___ 27. We should support our country, right or wrong.

___ 28. Some of the ideals of communism are worth working for.

___ 29. The foreign policy of all nations, including the U.S., is motivated primarily by selfish interest.

___ 30. Attempts to abolish war are idealistic and impractical.

___ 31. There is very little in the U.S. that I would want to change.

Chapter

Nationalism

Black Nationalism:
Racial Separation
in America

Viewpoint

The United States:
The Argument
for Black Separatism

Robert S. Browne

An economist, Robert S. Browne has worked
with the United States Foreign Aid Program
and taught at Fairleigh Dickenson University.
He is currently director of the Black Economic
Research Center and a member of the board of
directors of the American Committee on Africa.
The editor of *Review of Black Political
Economy*, he has written *Race Relations In
International Affairs* (1961) and *The Social
Scene* (1972).

Consider the following questions while reading:

1. In what ways do separatists and integrationists disagree?
2. How is a black person classed in America?
3. What arguments are given in support of black separatism?

Robert S. Browne, ''The Case for Two Americas — One Black, One White,'' **New York Times
Magazine**, August 11, 1968, pp. 12, 13, 50, 51, 56, 60. © 1968 by The New York Times
Company. Reprinted by permission.

SEPARATISM VERSUS INTEGRATION

A growing ambivalence among Negroes is creating a great deal of confusion both within the black community itself and within those segments of the white community that are attempting to relate to the blacks. It arises from the question of whether American Negroes are a cultural group significantly distinct from the majority culture *on an ethnic* rather than a socio-economic basis.

If one believes the answer to this is yes, one is likely to favor the cultural distinctiveness and to vigorously oppose efforts to minimize or submerge the differences. If, on the other hand, one believes there are no cultural differences between blacks and whites or that the differences are minimal or transitory, then one is likely to resist emphasis on the differences and to favor accentuation of the similarities. Those two currents in the black community are symbolized, perhaps oversimplified, by the factional labels of separatists and integrationists.

The separatist would argue that the Negro's foremost grievance cannot be solved by giving him access to more gadgets — although this is certainly a part of the solution — but that his greatest need is of the spirit, that he must have an opportunity to reclaim his group individuality and have that individuality recognized as equal with other major cultural groups in the world.

The integrationist would argue that what the Negro wants, principally, is exactly what the whites want — that is, to be ''in'' in American society — and that operationally this means providing the Negro with employment, income, housing and education comparable to that of the whites. Having achieved this, the other aspects of the Negro's problem of inferiority will disappear.

The origins of this dichotomy are easily identified. The physical characteristics which distinguish blacks from whites are obvious enough; the long history of slavery and the post-emancipation exclusion of the blacks from so many facets of American society are equally undeniable. Whether observable behavioral differences between blacks and the white majority are attributable to this special history of the black man in

America or to racial differences in life style is arguable. What is not arguable, however, is that at the time of the slave trade, the blacks arrived in America with a cultural background and life style quite distinct from that of the whites. Although there was perhaps as much diversity among these Africans from widely scattered portions of their native continent as there was among the settlers from Europe, the differences between the two racial groups was unquestionably far greater, as attested by the different roles they were to play in the society.

Over this history there seems to be little disagreement. The dispute arises from how one views what happened after the blacks reached this continent. The integrationist would focus on their transformation into imitators of the European civilization. European clothing was imposed on the slaves, eventually their languages were forgotten, the African homeland receded ever further into the background.

Certainly after 1808, when the slave trade was officially terminated, thus cutting off fresh injections of African culture, the Europeanizing of the blacks proceeded apace. With emancipation, the Federal Constitution recognized the legal manhood of the blacks, citizenship was conferred on the ex-slave, and the Negro began his arduous struggle for social, economic and political acceptance into the American mainstream.

The separatist, however, takes the position that the cultural transformation of the black man was not complete whereas the integrationist more or less accepts the destruction of the original culture of the African slaves as a *fait accompli* — whether he feels it to have been morally reprehensible or not — the separatist is likely to harbor a vague resentment toward the whites for having perpetrated this cultural genocide; he would nurture whatever vestiges may have survived the North American experience and would encourage a renaissance of these lost characteristics. In effect, he is sensitive to an identity crisis which presumably does not exist in the mind of the integrationist.

The separatist appears to be romantic and even reactionary to many observers. On the other hand, his viewpoint squares with mankind's most fundamental instinct — the instinct for survival. With so powerful a stimulus, and with the oppressive tendencies of white society, one could have almost predicted the emergence of the black separatist movement. Millions of black parents have been confronted with the poignant agony of raising black, kinky-haired children in a society where the standard of beauty is a milk-white skin and long, straight hair. To convince a black child that she is beautiful when every channel of value formation in the society is telling her the opposite is a heart-rending and well-nigh impossible task.

BLACK IS BEAUTIFUL

It is a challenge which confronts all Negroes, irrespective of their social and economic class, but the difficulty of dealing with it is likely to vary with the degree to which the family leads an integrated existence. A black child in a predominantly black school may realize that she doesn't look like the pictures in the books, magazines and TV advertisements, but at least she looks like her schoolmates and neighbors. The black child in a predominantly white school and neighborhood lacks even this basis for identification.

This identity problem is, of course, not peculiar to the Negro, nor is it limited to questions of physical appearance. Minorities of all sorts encounter it in one form or another — the immigrant who speaks with an accent, the Jewish child who doesn't celebrate Christmas, the vegetarian who shuns meats. But for the Negro the problem has a special dimension, for in the American ethos a black man is not only "different," he is classed as ugly and inferior.

This is not an easy situation to deal with, and the manner in which a Negro chooses tc handle it will be both determined by, and a determinant of, his larger political outlook. He can deal with it as a integrationist, accepting his child as being ugly by prevailing standards and urging him to excel in other ways to prove his worth; or he can deal with it as a black nationalist, telling the child that he is not a freak but rather part of a larger international community of black-skinned, kinky-haired people who have a beauty of their own, a glorious history and a great future....

SEPARATE NEGRO TOWNS

Well, we're in favor of giving them New York and New Jersey....Truth of the matter is, the idea is sound. But how you going to accomplish it after you've got this far along and have this many roots planted? To get people to up and walk off and leave a territory is going to be difficult to do. Theoretically, it's a good idea though....Separate Negro towns might be another solution. I think they ought to have their own council, own mayor, own police force. I don't think there's any objection to it. I think it's got to come.

Roy Harris, a segregationist and president of the Augusta, Georgia Citizens Council of America, upon being informed that the Black Nationalists want Georgia as part of their nation. Quoted in **Esquire Magazine**, January, 1969.

AFRICA IS NOT THE ANSWER

It has been marveled that we American Negroes, almost alone among the cultural groups of the world, exhibit no sense of nationhood. Perhaps it is true that we lack this sense, but there seems little doubt that the absence of a homeland exacts a severe if unconscious price from our psyche. Theoretically our homeland is the U.S.A. We pledge allegiance to the Stars and Stripes and sing the national anthem. But from the age when we first begin to sense that we are somehow "different," that we are victimized, these rituals begin to mean less to us than to our white compatriots. For many of us they become form without substance; for others they become a cruel and bitter mockery of our dignity and good sense; for relatively few of us do they retain a significance in any way comparable to their hold on our white brethren.

The recent coming into independence of many African states stimulated some speculation among Negroes that independent Africa might become the homeland they so desperately needed. A few made the journey and experienced a newly found sense of community and racial dignity. For many who went, however, the gratifying racial fraternity which they experienced was insufficient to compensate for the cultural estrangement accompanying it. They had been away from Africa too long and the differences in language, food and custom barred them from the "at home" feeling they were eagerly seeking. Symbolically, independent Africa could serve them as a homeland; practically, it could not. Their search continues — a search for a place where they can experience the security which comes from being a part of the majority culture, free at last from the inhibiting effects of cultural repression, from cultural timidity and shame.

AN AMERICAN HOMELAND

If we have been separated from Africa for so long that we are no longer quite at ease there, we are left with only one place to make our home, and that is in this land to which we were brought in chains. Justice would indicate such a solution in any case, for it is North America, not Africa, into which our toil and effort have been poured. This land is our rightful home and we are well within our rights in demanding an opportunity to enjoy it on the same terms as the other immigrants who have helped to develop it. Since few whites will deny the justice of this claim, it is paradoxical that we are offerred the option of exercising this birthright only on the condition that we abandon our culture, deny our race and integrate ourselves into the white community.

The "accepted" Negro, the "integrated" Negro are mere euphemisms which hide a cruel and relentless cultural destruction that is sometimes agonizing to the middle-class Negro but is becoming intolerable to the black masses. A Negro who refuses to yield his identity and to ape the white model finds he can survive in dignity only by rejecting the entire white society, which must ultimately mean challenging the law and the law-enforcement mechanisms. On the other hand, if he abandons his cultural heritage and succumbs to the lure of integration, he risks certain rejection and humiliation along the way, with absolutely no guarantee of ever achieving complete acceptance. That such unsatisfactory options are leading to almost continuous disruption and dislocation of our society should hardly be cause for surprise.

PARTITION THE UNITED STATES

A formal partitioning of the United States into two totally separate and independent nations, one white and one black, offers one way out of this tragic situation. Many will condemn it as a defeatist solution, but what they see as defeatism may better be described as a frank facing up to the realities of American society. A society is stable only to the extent that there exists a basic core of value judgments that are unthinkingly accepted by the great bulk of its members. Increasingly, Negroes are demonstrating that they do not accept the common core of values which underlies America, either because they had little to do with drafting it or because they feel it is weighted against their interests. The alleged disproportionately large number of Negro law violators, of unwed mothers, of illegitimate children, of nonworking adults *may* be indicators that there is no community of values such as has been supposed, although I am not unaware of racial socio-economic reasons for these statistics also.

But whatever the reason for observed behavioral differences, there is clearly no reason *why* the Negro should not have his own ideas about what the societal organization should be. The Anglo-Saxon system of organizing human relationships has certainly not proved itself to be superior to all other systems, and the Negro is likely to be more acutely aware of this fact than are most Americans.

Certainly partition would entail enormous initial hardships. But these difficulties and these hardships should be weighed against the prospects of prolonged and intensified racial strife stretching for years into the future. Indeed, the social fabric of America is far more likely to be able to withstand the strains of a partitioning of the country than those of an extended race war.

Viewpoint

The United States:
The Argument Against
Black Separatism

Bayard Rustin

A recipient of the Family of Man award by the
National Council of Churches (1968), Bayard
Rustin is one of the leading civil rights activists
in the United States. He was Field Secretary for
the Congress of Racial Equality (1941), Special
Assistant to Dr. Martin Luther King Jr. (1955-
1960) and has held several other positions with
civil rights organizations. An advocate of non-
violence and constitutional methods of reform,
Rustin has authored *Down the Line* (1971) and
numerous articles.

Consider the following questions while reading:

1. Why is black separatism unrealistic?
2. What is reverse-ism?
3. What kind of action should blacks take?

Bayard Rustin, ''Towards Integration As A Goal,'' **AFL-CIO American Federationist**, January
1969, pp. 5-7. Reprinted with permission.

SEPARATION: A FRUSTRATION REACTION

The proposition that separation may be the best solution of America's racial problems has been recurrent in American Negro history....

Today, we are experiencing the familiar syndrome again. The Civil Rights Acts of 1964 and 1965 and the Supreme Court decisions all led people seriously to believe that progress was forthcoming, as they believed the day Martin Luther King said, "I have a dream." What made the March on Washington in 1963 great was the fact that it was the culmination of a period of great hope and anticipation.

But what has happened since? The ghettos are fuller than they have ever been, with 500,000 people moving into them each year and only some 40,000 moving out. They are the same old Bedford-Stuyvesant, Harlem, Detroit and Watts, only they are much bigger, with more rats, more roaches and more despair.

There are more Negro youngsters in segregated schoolrooms than there were in 1954 — not all due to segregation or discrimination, perhaps, but a fact. The number of youngsters who have fallen back in their reading, writing and arithmetic since 1954 has increased, not decreased, and unemployment for Negro young women is up to 35, 40 and 50 percent in the ghettos. For young men in the ghettos, it is up to 20 percent and this is a conservative figure. For family men, the unemployment is twice that of whites. Having built up hopes, and suffered the despair which followed, we are again in a period where separation is being discussed.

I maintain that, in all three periods, the turn to separation has been a frustration reaction to objective political, social and economic circumstances. I believe that it is fully justified, for it would be the most egregious wishful thinking to suppose that people can be subjected to deep frustration and yet not act in a frustrated manner.

But however justified and inevitable the frustration, it is totally unrealistic to divert the attention of young Negroes at this time either to the idea of a separate state in the United States, or to going back to Africa, or to setting up a black capitalism (as Mr.

Nixon and CORE are now advocating), or to talk about any other possibility of economic separation, when those Negroes who are well off are the 2 million Negroes who are integrated into the trade union movement.

This is not to belittle in any way the desirability of fostering a sense of ethnic unity or racial pride among Negroes or relationships to other black people around the world. This is all to the good, but the ability to do this in a healthy rather than a frustrated way will depend upon the economic viability of the Negro community, the degree to which it can participate in the democratic process here rather than separate from it, and the degree to which it accepts methods of struggle that are productive....

BLACK NATIONALISM AND "REVERSE-ISM"

To return to separation and nationalism. We must distinguish within this movement that which is unsound from that which is sound, for ultimately no propaganda can work for social change which is not based in absolute psychological truth.

There is an aspect of the present thrust toward black nationalism that I call reverse-ism. This is dangerous. Black people now want to argue that their hair is beautiful. All right. It is truthful and useful. But, to the degree that the nationalist movement takes concepts of reaction and turns them upside down and paints them glorious for no other reason than that they are black, we're in trouble — morally and politically. The Ku Klux Klan used to say: "If you're white, you're right; if you're black, no matter who you are, you're no good." And there are those among us who are now saying the opposite of the Ku Klux Klan: "He's a whitey, he's no good."

The Ku Klux Klan said: "You know, we can't have black people teaching" and they put up a big fight when the first Negro was hired in a white school in North Carolina. Now, for all kinds of "glorious" reasons, we're turning that old idea upside down and saying: "Well, somehow or other, there's soul involved and only black teachers can teach black children." But it is not true. Good teachers can teach children.

The Ku Klux Klan said: "We don't want you in our community; get out." Now there are blacks saying: "We don't want any

whites in our community for business or anything; get out."
The Ku Klux Klan said: "We will be violent as a means of impressing our will on the situation." And now, in conference after conference, a small number of black people use violence and threats to attempt to obstruct the democratic process.

NEW POLITICAL COMMUNITIES

The black rural enclaves and urban ghettos cannot create a new nation, but they can attempt to form a new type of local political community....The critical problem at this stage is whether the new political communities, whatever they may be, will relate more or less realistically to the rest of the country or whether they will be infected with the nationalist fantasy and encourage a destructive — and self-destructive — separation from the rest of the country.

Theodore Draper, "The Fantasy of Black Nationalism," **Commentary**, September, 1969.

DOMINANCE OF CLASS OVER COLOR

What is essential and what we must not lose sight of is that true self-respect and a true sense of image are the results of a social process and not merely a psychological state of mind.

It is utterly unrealistic to expect the Negro middle class to behave on the basis alone of color. They will behave, first of all, as middle-class people. The minute Jews got enough money to move off Allen Street, they went to West End Avenue. As soon as the Irish could get out of Hell's Kitchen, they beat it to what is now Harlem. Who thinks the Negro middle classes are going to stay in Harlem? I believe that the fundamental mistake of the nationalist movement is that it does not comprehend that class ultimately is a more driving force than color and that any effort to build a society for American Negroes that is based on color alone is doomed to failure.

A PATH TO THE FUTURE

Now, there are several possibilities. One possibility is that we can stay here and continue the struggle; sometimes things will be better, sometimes they will be worse. Another is to separate ourselves into our own state in America. But I reject that because I do not believe that the American government will ever accept it. Thirdly, there is a possibility of going back to Africa and that is out for me, because I've had enough experience with the Africans to know that they will not accept that.

There is a kind of in-between position — stay here and try to separate and yet not separate. I tend to believe that both have to go on simultaneously. That is to say, there has to be a move on the part of Negroes to develop black institutions and a black image, and all this has to go on while they are going downtown into integrated work situations, while they are trying to get into the suburbs if they can, while they are doing what all other Americans do in their economic and social grasshopping. That is precisely what the Jew has done. He has held on to that which is Jewish, and nobody has made a better effort at integrating out there and making sure that he's out there where the action is. It makes for tensions, but I don't believe there's any other viable reality.

Furthermore, I believe that the most important thing for those of us in the trade union movement, in the religious communities and in the universities is not to be taken in by methods that appeal to people's viscera but do not in fact solve the problems that stimulated their viscera.

We must fight and work for a social and economic program which will lift America's poor, whereby the Negro who is most grievously poor will be lifted to that position where he will be able to have dignity.

Secondly, we must fight vigorously for Negroes to engage in the political process, since there is only one way to have maximum feasible participation — and that is not by silly little committees deciding what they're going to do with a half million dollars, but by getting out into the real world of politics and making their weight felt. The most important thing that we have to do is to restore a sense of dignity to the Negro people.

If that can happen, the intense frustration around the problem of separation will decrease as equal opportunities — economic, political and social — increase. And that is the choice before us.

Viewpoint  13

Black Americans:
Captives of War

Muhammad Ahmad

Supporters of national independence for
America's blacks base their argument upon the
premise that the political, social, and economic
institutions of the United States are primarily
racist. Since more than 100 years of "freedom"
has failed to truly liberate blacks, it is main-
tained that the only viable alternative is to
establish a separate national identity. The following reading, by Muhammad Ahmad, appeared in *The Black Scholar*, October, 1972. In
it, Ahmad contends that America's blacks are a
"captive colonial nation" and that emancipation can be achieved by disrupting the oppressive political system.

Consider the following questions while reading:

1. What does Ahmad mean by the phrase "captives of war"?
2. Why does he say that "every African person in America is...
   in prison."?
3. What is the Amen-Ra method?

Muhammad Ahmad, "We Are All Prisoners of War," **Black Scholar**, October 1972, pp. 3-5.
Reprinted by permission.

The time has come for us to stand up as men and women, *unite* and organize ourselves against every racist attack unleashed on us....

Our movement recognizes that we are a captive colonial nation, therefore, we see the legal and political system being a racist colonial ill-legal system. We declare our independence from the system.

We want national independence by any means necessary. The war prisoners movement is the broad united front of our nationalist revolution. Our movement calls upon all Africans to *unite* regardless of ideology and religion. To move to self reliance we must have a national black united front. But unity must be based on principle and actions, and not words alone.

When we say, ''We want freedom for all black people held in federal, state, county and city prisons and jails. We believe under the present system that no black people have received a fair and impartial trial. We believe that this racist system is organized in all ways against black people...'', we feel *there are no laws in America that African peoples need to abide by until we have the right to determine our own destinies.*

We say this because we recognize that we (African people in America) are not citizens denied our rights but we are captives of war. War was declared on the African nation 500 years ago and has not stopped yet. If we are not captives of war, then we wouldn't be in America. We would still be in Africa.

There is no such thing as a second class citizen. *A second class citizen is a 20th century slave.* You are either a first class citizen or a ward of the state, which means no class at all — it means captive. We are forced to abide by the responsibilities of citizenship but are denied the equal rights of citizens. So, our status has changed from chattel slavery to citizen slavery. After the signing of the Emancipation Proclamation, which supposedly made us freedmen, a vote was never taken to see whether we wanted to be citizens of the kidnapper government, return to our motherland or whether we wanted land right here. So, the so-called citizenship that we are supposed to have, but don't enjoy, is a forced citizenship and is therefore ill-legal, making our status colonial subjects held in captivity. Every African person in America is therefore in prison.

We, as a people/nation, will not have the status of freedmen or women until we secure the right to determine our own destiny. Until African people have the right to self determination, *America is a police state to 30 million Africans*....

In order to advance the Pan-African revolution, from working together regardless of ideology, we must develop a style of work which is effective in mobilizing the millions of our people. We call this work style, the Amen-Ra (RAM) method. It is the building of cells among the people, quietly working on community problems and projects, working towards the emergence of a Pan-African Nationalist Party.

The Pan-African movement in America in many respects is still

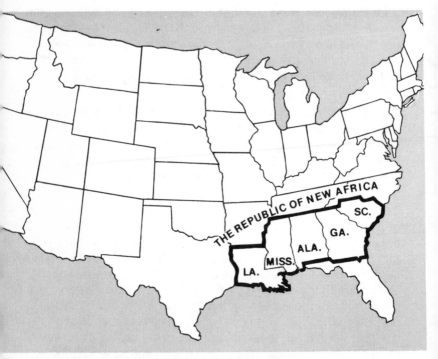

Robert F. William's projected Republic of New Africa, "a nation within nations"

a petty bourgeois movement. There are still many utopian concepts in the movement such as the fantasies of ''going back to Africa'' and ''ego tripping on messianic cultural nationalism.''

Culture is important but it is not the predominating factor in a revolution. *Political development of the masses is the central factor in a revolution.* Mass mobilization that disrupts and overturns a system is the heart of a revolution.

THE REPUBLIC OF NEW AFRICA

The concept of the Republic of New Africa is not a segregationist concept, but rather one of self-determination for an oppressed people. It represents a rallying point for progressive and constructive Black Nationalism.

Robert F. Williams, a Black separatist and President of the projected Republic of New Africa.

The war prisoners movement means Pan-African nationalists must move in a new direction. We must move to unite with the overall majority of the people.

We must move to have mass demonstrations in support of African captive prisoners. The war prisoners movement must not be separated from other direct actions over community issues. The struggle for community control of schools, Black Studies and African Liberation Day must be welded into one movement. The Pan-African movement must be action-oriented. While we build independent nationalist institutions we must move and dislocate the enemy's institutions.

We must move to disrupt the political system by starting an *African Independence Political Movement.*

A "New" Republic
of the United States

Martin Luther King, Jr.

Until his assassination in 1968, Martin Luther
King, Jr. led the movement for nonviolent
resistance to racial segregation and discrimination in the United States. An ordained minister
and gifted orator who appealed to peoples of
all colors and classes, he was instrumental in
forming the Southern Christian Leadership
Conference which worked with local black
leaders to speed desegregation. King's fame
and influence reached far beyond his native
America and in 1964 he was awarded the Nobel
Prize for Peace.

Consider the following questions while reading:

1. What promissory note has America defaulted on?
2. What tactics should be used to promote racial justice?
3. What is King's dream?

From Martin Luther King's **I Have A Dream** speech.

COLLECTING A DEBT

Five score years ago, a great American, in whose symbolic shadow we stand today, signed the Emancipation Proclamation. This momentous decree came as a great beacon of hope to millions of slaves, who had been seared in the flames of withering injustice. It came as a joyous daybreak to end the long night of their captivity.

But one hundred years later the colored American is still not free. One hundred years later the life of the colored American is still sadly crippled by the manacle of segregation and the chains of discrimination.

One hundred years later the colored American lives on a lonely island of poverty in the midst of a vast ocean of material prosperity. One hundred years later, the colored American is still languishing in the corners of American society and finds himself an exile in his own land. So we have come here today to dramatize a shameful condition.

In a sense we have come to our Nation's Capital to cash a check. When the architects of our great republic wrote the magnificent words of the Constitution and the Declaration of Independence, they were signing a promissory note to which every American was to fall heir.

This note was a promise that all men, yes, black men as well as white men, would be guaranteed the inalienable rights of life, liberty, and the pursuit of happiness.

It is obvious today that America has defaulted on this promissory note insofar as her citizens of color are concerned. Instead of honoring this sacred obligation, America has given its colored people a bad check, a check that has come back marked ''insufficient funds.''

But we refuse to believe that the bank of justice is bankrupt. We refuse to believe that there are insufficient funds in the great vaults of opportunity of this nation. So we have come to cash this check, a check that will give us upon demand the riches of freedom and security of justice.

BLACKS AND WHITES TOGETHER

We have also come to this hallowed spot to remind America of the fierce urgency of *Now*. This is no time to engage in the luxury of cooling off or to take the tranquilizing drug of gradualism.

Now is the time to make real the promise of democracy.

Now is the time to rise from the dark and desolate valley of segregation to the sunlit path of racial justice.

Now is the time to lift our nation from the quicksands of racial injustice to the solid rock of brotherhood.

Now is the time to make justice a reality to all of God's children....There will be neither rest nor tranquillity in America until the color citizen is granted his citizenship rights. The whirlwinds of revolt will continue to shake the foundations of our nation until the bright day of justice emerges.

But there is something that I must say to my people who stand on the threshold which leads into the palace of justice. In the process of gaining our rightful place we must not be guilty of wrongful deeds.

Let us not seek to satisfy our thirst for freedom by drinking from the cup of bitterness and hatred.

We must forever conduct our struggle on the high plane of dignity and discipline. We must not allow our creative protest to degenerate into physical violence.

Again and again we must rise to the majestic heights of meeting physical force with soul force. The marvelous new militancy which has engulfed the colored community must not lead us to a distrust of all white people, for many of our white brothers, evidenced by their presence here today, have come to realize that their destiny is tied up with our destiny and their freedom is inextricably bound to our freedom.

We cannot walk alone....

ALL MEN ARE EQUAL

I have a dream that one day this nation will rise up and live out the true meaning of its creed. We hold these truths to be self-evident that all men are created equal.

"I HAVE A DREAM TODAY"

I still have a dream. It is a dream deeply rooted in the American dream.

I have a dream that one day this nation will rise up and live out the true meaning of its creed. We hold these truths to be self-evident that all men are created equal.

I have a dream that one day out in the red hills of Georgia the sons of former slaves and the sons of former slaveowners will be able to sit down together at the table of brotherhood....

I have a dream that my four little children will one day live in a nation where they will not be judged by the color of their skin but by their character.

I have a dream today.

I have a dream that one day down in Alabama, with its vicious racists, with its governor having his lips dripping with the words of interposition and nullification; that one day right down in Alabama little black boys and black girls will be able to join hands with little white boys and white girls as sisters and brothers.

I have a dream today.

I have a dream that one day every valley shall be engulfed, every hill shall be exalted, and every mountain shall be made low, the rough places will be made plains, and the crooked places will be made straight, and the glory of the Lord shall be revealed and all flesh shall see it together.

This is our hope. This is the faith that I will go back to the South with. With this faith we will be able to hew out of the mountain of despair a stone of hope.

With this faith we will be able to transform the jangling discords of our nation into a beautiful symphony of brotherhood.

With this faith we will be able to work together, to pray together, to struggle together, to go to jail together, to climb up for freedom together, knowing that we will be free one day.

This will be the day when all of God's children will be able to sing with new meaning ''My country 'tis of thee, sweet land of liberty, of thee I sing. Land where my fathers died, land of the Pilgrim's pride, from every mountainside, let freedom ring!''

And if America is to be a great nation, this must become true. So, let freedom ring from the hilltops of New Hampshire. Let freedom ring from the mighty mountains of New York.

''I have a dream'': Martin Luther King, Jr., speaks at the Lincoln Memorial, 1963. United Press International, Inc.

Let freedom ring from the heightening Alleghenies of Pennsylvania.

Let freedom ring from the snow-capped Rockies of Colorado.

Let freedom ring from the curvacious slopes of California.

But not only that, let freedom ring from the Stone Mountain of Georgia.

Let freedom ring from every hill and molehill of Mississippi and every mountainside.

When we let freedom ring, when we let it ring from every tenement and every hamlet, from every state and city, we will be able to speed up that day when all of God's children, black men and white men, Jews and Gentiles, Protestants and Catholics, will be able to join hands and sing in the words of the old spiritual, ''Free at last, free at last? Thank God Almighty, we are free at last.''

Distinguishing Between Bias, Fact and Reason

Instructions

One of the most important critical thinking skills is the ability to distinguish between opinions based on emotions or bias and those based on rational consideration of the facts. This activity is designed to promote experimentation with one's capacity to distinguish between emotional or biased statements, rational statements and statements of fact.

Examine the following statements. Mark (R) for any statement that you think is based on a rational consideration of the facts. Mark (B) for any statement you believe is based on bias or emotion. Mark (F) for any sentence you think is a statement of fact. Then discuss and compare your judgments with other class members.

> **B = A statement based on bias**
> **R = A statement based on reason**
> **F = A statement of fact**

_____ 1. Many American schools have not been desegregated.

_____ 2. Jews have many irritating habits and manners.

_____ 3. Blacks are mostly to blame for their social and economic problems.

_____ 4. White people are more likely to succeed in education.

_____ 5. Black people often lack initiative and dependability.

_____ 6. Europeans are very ambitious, capable and intelligent.

_____ 7. Christians are morally superior to other people.

_____ 8. Jews quite often become wealthy by manipulating others.

_____ 9. Democratic nations have fought only defensive wars.

_____ 10. Internal social problems are the biggest threat to American security.

_____ 11. Italians are more prone to crime and violence than other people.

_____ 12. Indians tend to lack initiative and independence.

_____ 13. In the last fifteen years, the U.S. has made progress in the fight against racial discrimination.

_____ 14. Black families should not try to force themselves into white neighborhoods.

_____ 15. Segregated neighborhoods promote less conflict and are better for blacks and whites.

_____ 16. Busing to promote integrated schools should not be forced on people who don't want it.

_____ 17. White people will seek to exploit others.

_____ 18. Black people have superior athletic and musical talents.

_____ 19. Indians are similar in behavior to other people.

_____ 20. Chicanos are as friendly as other people.

_____ 21. Indians must be dealt with forcefully since democratic procedures will never make them behave properly.

_____ 22. Jews usually interfere too much with other people's business.

_____ 23. It would be unreasonable to blame white people for racial conflict in America.

_____ 24. The government of South Africa administers a policy of racial separation called apartheid.

_____ 25. The nuclear arms race threatens the safety and survival of all people.

_____ 26. Jews have money and power out of proportion to their numbers.

_____ 27. Black separatism is no more of an answer to our racial problems than white separatism.

_____ 28. Racial conflict is America's most serious internal problem.

_____ 29. American military intervention in Vietnam was unjustified.

Chapter 4

Nationalism

American Nationalism:
A Time for Change?

INTRODUCTION

By and large, nationalism in the United States is a unique phenomenon. The mixed ethnic nature of American society and the lack of a common cultural and historical tradition account for this. In the broadest sense, all Americans (Native Americans excepted) are American by adoption, rather than birth. Although English is their universal language, a majority of Americans can claim other than English ancestry. Moreover, the United States is a relatively young country. While Italy, Greece, Egypt, Persia, China, and a host of other nations can boast of a history which traces to antiquity, America has enjoyed a sovereign heritage of only two hundred years. As many professors of ancient history are fond of repeating, it took the Roman Empire longer to decline and fall than America is old.

It is America's reverent regard for the democratic ideal which both defines American nationalism and lends it its peculiar character. All Americans have been nurtured on the democratic principles of self-determination and equality of rights and instructed on the means and necessity of preserving them. Thus it is not so much the flag to which Americans pledge their allegiance but the credo it represents. Indeed, democracy seems to be the single national theme with which this mixed society can identify in the absence of a time-honored and common cultural tradition.

America's military involvements illustrate the unusual nature of American nationalism. Although not seriously threatened by foreign invasion since the War of 1812, the United States nonetheless has been directly involved in several international and local conflicts. In each case, (the Spanish-American War, World Wars I and II, the Korean War, the Vietnamese War) the defense of freedom, not the motherland, was the alleged factor motivating involvement. By "making the world safe for democracy," Americans were, by logical extension, keeping democracy safe at home.

Vietnam proved to be the ordeal by fire for traditional nationalism as the war prompted many to examine the ultimate sources and grounds of American democracy. For the first time, the morality and designs of an American military involvement were seriously questioned on a large and telling scale. In daily newspaper editorials, in college and high school classrooms, from church pulpits, and down to that most basic unit of Americana, the family evening meal, the same questions were being asked with a growing and monotonous regularity. Was the cause of freedom at home and in the world really being served in Vietnam or had the United States government created a self-serving illusion? Did America possess the economic and military resources to oversee world freedom; and, more basically, did it hold the moral right? And as a final, scathing indictment, was American interventionism abroad anything but hypocritical so long as the nation continued to ally with and even underwrite dictatorial regimes whose dubious saving grace was their opposition to communism?

The immediate issue of the war itself ended when the last American solider left Vietnam in 1973. However, the debate generated by it continues and there are strong indications that the final outcome will be a substantive shift in the essence and disposition of American nationalism.

Although not all of the following readings deal either directly or indirectly with Vietnam, the challenge to traditional American nationalism which grew out of the war is apparent in most of them. The readings by John E. Davis and Melvin Munn betray a concern that widespread domestic opposition to the foreign policies of the United States might decidedly undermine national security. Also present is the familiar call to maintain a militarily strong and ideologically cohesive America in order to preserve freedom at home and abroad. The opposing viewpoints represent three of the more prevalent contemporary challenges to traditional nationalism — neo-isolationism, socialism and internationalism.

Viewpoint  15

What is Patriotism?

The Associated Press

The following article is an Associated Press
Newsfeature which appeared in the *San Diego
Union* on December 14, 1969. It illustrates the
range of attitudes toward patriotism* generated
by American involvement in Vietnam.

Consider the following questions while reading:

1. In what different ways can patriotism be defined?
2. How can symbols be misused?

*Webster's New World Dictionary of the American Language defines
patriotism as ''love and loyal or zealous support of one's own country,
especially in all matters involving other countries; [also] nationalism.''

Associated Press, ''New Patriotic Feeling Rises,'' **San Diego Union**, December 14, 1969.
Reprinted with permission.

From its lofty isolation on a windless moon to an endless, earthly vigil over a thousand city halls, the American flag is getting around nowadays.

On car bumpers, car windows, car aerials, car doors.

In stores, in homes, in churches, in halls.

It's there, almost everywhere, a mute symbol of America...and some highly contradictory ideas.

"I consider the flag as sacred as the sacraments of my church," says an Elks lodge official. "Anyone who would destroy it is stupid."

"The flag," counters a Negro poverty worker, "never did anything for anybody. Try to find one in the black ghetto."

The alienated, peace-beaded hippie?

"Countries cause all our problems," says one. "I don't believe in flags."

ADDS UP TO PATRIOTISM

Sacred, suspected and a little over-simplified. It all adds up to that perplexing expression called patriotism.

Patriotism?

For some, it is supporting the government in the face of criticism, and for others it is criticizing the government to speed reforms.

For some, it is mounting the drive for law and order, and for others it's breaking the law to further a cause.

Historically, a patriot was that person who loved his country and promoted and defended its interests. And historically, as now, almost anyone could qualify as long as national interest remained a matter of personal persuasion.

Who, then, is a patriot?

The next best question, with more available answers, is how and why are Americans patriotic.

"I've always gone back to the fundamental that action brings reaction," says Frank Wetzel, a director of the U.S. Flag Foundation in New York.

"There's a new feeling of patriotism today because people are tired of protests. They're starting to collect their ideas and take a stand."

Patriotism in the past two years has been a highly visual expression. And it has been something of a phenomenon.

Actor Chuck Connors helps raise flag at spot where Vietnam protesters had earlier burned one, 1967. Wide World Photos

Reader's Digest, in a spectacularly successful campaign started last February, distributed more than 18 million flag decals to its subscribers, then was flooded with requests for 32 million more.

Most of the additional decals went to large corporations, including Gulf Oil Co., which is handing out more than 20 million of the flag stickers as a service station promotion.

LOVE IT OR LEAVE

Another popular decal — an Elks' sticker bearing the slogan "Our Flag — Love It or Leave" — was first distributed through local lodges a year ago and has topped one million in circulation.

Boston policeman retrieves flag set afire to protest American role in Vietnam, 1971. United Press International, Inc.

New York's Daily News has distributed more than one million flag stickers to its readership, including one designed in honor of the Apollo 11 moon mission and carrying the slogan, ''Good Old USA.''

Since most of the decals were distributed at no cost and without request, it is difficult to measure public response to the flag campaigns. However, it is overwhelming if it is anything like the demand for cloth flags.

New York's Annin Flag Co., one of the country's oldest and largest flag manufacturers, has had its orders doubled in the last year.

''The demand is incredible, especially for flags that you attach to car aerials,'' said a spokesman. ''I suppose it's all part of the new conservative trend in the country, a reaction to all the protests.''

''Patriotism is a word monopolized by the right, and in the rightest view, it involves a sort of mindless allegiance based on accident of birth,'' says Ira Glasser, staff attorney for the American Civil Liberties Union in New York.

''It's translated into a belief that unpopular views must be suppressed,'' he said. ''And it has little to do with values underlying the Bill of Rights.''

Glasser, who specializes in court action involving student protestors, is most concerned about application of patriotic symbols to law and order issues.

SYMBOLS MISUSED

''It's frightening that good people can end up subscribing to totalitarianism through misuse of patriotic symbols,'' he said, ''but that is exactly what's happening.''

Whether or not the ambitions of the New Left are patriotic concerns practically no one inside the movement.

But, for the sake of argument, young radicals see nothing about their thinking that isn't patriotic.

"The New Left is an authentically American development," says Dave Gelber, 28, an editorial associate of New York's Liberation magazine, a forum for leftist organizations.

"American radicals couldn't conceive of any other country to live in other than their own," he said. "They want to stay in this country. They want to make something that is decent and livable."

Then there is Barbara Crane, a Clinton, N.Y., mother who has decals on her car, plus an aerial flag, and who organized a counter-protest to protest the anti-Vietnam war protest.

Viewpoint  16

The "Old" Patriotism

John E. Davis

John E. Davis is a former Director of Civil
Defense with the Office of the Secretary of the
Army and former Director of the Civil Preparedness Agency with the Department of Defense. A
highly decorated World War II veteran, he is a
member of the Veterans of Foreign Wars and
the American Legion (National Commander
1966-1967). While serving as National Commander, Davis delivered the following address
at the Los Angeles Bowl Luncheon on January
3, 1967.

Consider the following questions while reading:

1. What is the most demanding responsibility of citizenship?
2. How does Davis describe the elements of citizenship?

John E. Davis, "What Should An American Citizen Be?" **Vital Speeches**, February 1, 1967, p.
238-40. Reprinted with permission.

OUR MEN IN VIETNAM

As many of you know, it was just three weeks ago that I set foot back on U.S. soil here in California following an extended tour of the Far East, and a part of that time overseas was spent with our armed forced in South Viet Nam. Since returning from the Orient, I have also been out of the country in the opposite direction visiting U.S. installations on the Caribbean Sea Frontier.

I'm delighted to report to you that the caliber of American military leadership in Viet Nam is superb, and the quality of our fighting men in every branch of the service is excellent — undoubtedly the finest we have ever put in the field.

Our effort in Viet Nam should be directed toward a successful conclusion to these hostilities as quickly as possible so we can bring these men back home.

Having seen young Americans serving on both sides of the world, one cannot help but be impressed with the spirit, the capabilities, the knowhow and the resourcefulness that American servicemen of today bring to the all important job of defending freedom....

RESPONSIBILITIES OF AMERICAN CITIZENSHIP

It was Alexander Hamilton who said: "Those who enjoy the fruits of democracy must be willing to bear arms in its defense," and, as I have mentioned I believe we are in agreement that this is the most demanding responsibility of citizenship.

Yet, it is a fact of life that there are those among us today who are all too willing to taste of the fruits of democracy and to enjoy the *rights* of citizenship, but who recoil in horror when it is suggested that they too must shoulder their share of citizenship *responsibility*.

Under the great spectacle of the Rose Bowl which unfolded here yesterday, where a few performed and millions watched, citizenship is not a spectator sport. The strength of freedom and its very survival depends upon a thoughtful and active citizenry, and everyone who is concerned with his personal future, with that of his family and that of his country, had better get in the game.

We seem to be faced with a strange and unwholesome paradox today in that we are sending young Americans ten thousand miles from home to fight, and perhaps to die, in the cause of freedom, while here on the home front we are all too apathetic and lethargic about preserving the very virtues and principles for which we are asking these men to risk their lives.

I think each one of us owes a great deal to these men, and the one method which each of us has at his command to express our appreciation is to stand up to the responsibilities of good citizenship, and to make sure they will come home to the kind of country and the type of a society in which they can take everlasting pride.

Sometimes I think that among our naturalized citizens we find a keener sense of citizenship responsibility than we do among many who are blessed with citizenship in the land of the free by virtue of birth. We may be assured that those who have known a different way of life in other lands, those who have been oppressed at the hands of tyrants, have a deeper appreciation of many of the blessings which we have come to take for granted.

LOVE OF COUNTRY

Each of these new citizens has had an indoctrination into our way of life, some phases of which the natural born have never known, and I suspect that one of the elements of that indoctrination that has escaped so many of our people is the American's Creed, written a half century ago by William Tyler Page, then Clerk of the United States House of Representatives. This is it:

"I believe in the United States of America as a Government of the people, by the people, for the people, whose just powers are derived from the consent of the governed; a democracy in a republic; a sovereign nation of many sovereign states; a perfect union, one and inseparable, established upon those principles of freedom, equality, justice and humanity for which American patriots sacrificed their lives and fortunes. I therefore believe it my duty to my country to love it, to support its Constitution, to obey its laws, to respect its flag, and to defend it against all enemies...."

Let's examine briefly the elements of citizenship as described in the Creed.

First, I believe it my duty to my country to love it. There are many ways in which an individual may express his love of country, and in many instances that love may manifest itself as much in the things as individual refrains from doing or saying as in those things which he does or says. For example: No right is absolute. While we cherish and defend the right of free speech, that right does not permit one to shout "fire" in a crowded auditorium, nor does it permit one to engage in libel or slander, or to incite to riot or insurrection. We believe every citizen must study and decide not what is best for himself or for a special interest group, but what is best for his country.

PROUD TO BE AN AMERICAN

We must realize that once truly implanted in the hearts and minds of the youth of this country, freedom will never die. Make them proud to be an American.

Roy W. Harper, Chief Judge, Eastern District of the United States, in a speech delivered to the "Backstoppers," St. Louis, Missouri, May 9, 1972.

RESPECT FOR "OLD GLORY"

We believe, as did William Tyler Page, that it is the duty of every citizen to uphold and defend the Constitution of The United States of America. This is the essential document which guarantees your freedoms and mine. It was never meant to provide a refuge for the lawless or a haven for those who would destroy it. Yet, there are those who, while openly advocating the overthrow of our government, claim the protection of the very instrument they would negate. Prominent among the offenders is the Community Party, USA. Its members and those who have been duped by its guile are the first to cry "persecution," and "violation of Constitutional rights," when brought before the bar of justice.

As citizens, we are expected to show due respect to our flag, for it is the symbol of everything we hold dear. More than a half million Americans have died in the defense of the principles and ideals which Old Glory symbolizes, yet we find those who willingly accept the protection and the blessings for which it stands but who refuse to raise a hand to salute it — much less to defend it. Worse still, there are a few of the despicable ones who would stoop to desecrate that glorious symbol. The American Legion vigorously supports legislation that would make such an act a federal offense, and we would ask that every offender be prosecuted to the full extent of such legislation.

WILLINGNESS TO DIE

Finally, we reach the ultimate demand of citizenship — to defend this country against all enemies. The American Legion believes it to be the responsibility of every able-bodied, mentally qualified, male citizen to bear arms in the defense of his country should the need arise. We do not believe that service in such areas as the Peace Corps or the Job Corps should be considered a substitute for military service.

An advertisement sponsored by Freedom House in the November 30 issue of the New York Times lists a number of

American Way Features

fantasies that should be renounced by the American people if we are interested in seeing the Viet Nam war concluded by a just peace.

Among them is this point: "That military service in this country's armed forces is an option exercisable solely at the discretion of the individual. No nation anywhere, now or in the past, has ever recognized that principle. Those who urge defiance on moral grounds merely betray the genuine tenets of conscientious objection which our people respect."

My friends, I have always been impressed with the wording of a prize winning essay, written by Ralph Bushnell Potts for the American Bar Association, on the subject of the responsibility of the citizen as a voter. The final sentence of Potts' message reads as follows: "I vote as if my ballot alone decided the contest. I may lose my preference, but I will not throw away my sacred vote. For within the booth I hold in my humble hands the living proxy of all my country's honorable dead."

In closing I make a humble effort to paraphrase that thought so beautifully expressed by the writer. I think each of us could say: "I will live my life as though my country's future depended upon me alone. I could lose my life, but I will not forfeit the precious heritage that is mine. I will not destroy by neglect, nor will I stand idly by and permit others to destroy this precious birthright. Within my home abide good citizens. I have helped to teach them the values by which to guide their lives. We are in accord that what we have is good. We will do what we must to preserve it."

The "New" Patriotism

Garry Wills

Garry Wills received his PhD from Yale University in 1961. He was an Assistant Professor of Classics at Johns Hopkins University from 1962 to 1967. Although a classicist by training, he has written extensively on contemporary political problems. The following excerpt from his *Nixon Agonistes* reveals a neo-isolationist attitude regarding Vietnam in particular, and United States foreign policy in general. In a review of the book in the Chicago Sun-Times, Wills was called "a gifted writer...describing the essential feel of America and the American people moving into the 1970's."

Consider the following questions while reading:

1. Why did Robert E. Lee fight for the South?
2. What is the only honorable motive for war?
3. What is the relationship between money for arms and food?

Garry Wills, **Nixon Agonistes** (Boston: Houghton Mifflin, 1969, 1970), pp. 440-42, 451.
Copyright © 1969, 1970 by Garry Wills. Reprinted by permission of Houghton Mifflin
Company.

LEE AND THE CIVIL WAR

Decatur's formula does not seem so unreasonable after all — especially when we recall its authentic form (so often misquoted): his toast was, ''Our country! In her intercourse with foreign nations may she always be in the right; but our country, right or wrong!'' Can that toast be a moral guide? Perhaps. Our history contains a famous instance of a man choosing his country though he knew her course was wrong. Colonel Robert E. Lee was no secessionist in 1860 — he said that if he owned all the slaves in the South, he would give them up to save the Union he had fought for. Yet, as a professional soldier, he had only three choices — (a) to remain in the federal army and help destroy his own state, in the process killing his friends, his relatives, the countrymen closest to him; or (b) to resign his commission and stand by idle, watching others ravage his homeland and kill his friends; or (c) though convinced of the futility of secession, to stand, once it came, between his people and those who would harm them. The first choice he had to reject (refusing, in the process, Lincoln's offer that he lead the new Union Army being raised). Having resigned his commission — he could not take part in preparations to invade his native state — he hoped that his military career was at an end, that the conflict would be averted and he could remain a civilian. It was in this period that he refused command of the new Comfederate army being raised. But when his native state seceded (men cheered crazily in the streets of Alexandria while Lee's Arlington home went into mourning), he could not refuse his governor's request that he lead the troops of Virginia. He chose his country, right or wrong — rather, he chose his country, wrong. It is impossible to think this an immoral decision, especially when we read the anguished letters he wrote to friends, justifying it.

LEE'S ANGUISH

With all my devotion to the Union and the feeling of loyalty and duty of an American citizen, I have not been able to make up my mind to raise my hand against my relatives, my children, my home. I have therefore resigned my commission in the Army, and save in defence of my native state, with the sincere hope that my poor services may never be needed, I hope I may never be called on to draw my sword.

After the most anxious inquiry as to the correct course for me to pursue, I concluded to resign…I am liable at any time to be ordered on duty, which I could not conscientiously perform….I am now a private citizen, and have no other ambition than to remain at home.

Tell Custis [his son, also in the army] he must consult his own judgment, reason and conscience as to the course he may take. I do not wish him to be guided by my wishes or example. If I have done wrong, let him do better.

COUNTRY OR COUNTRYMEN

It might be objected that Lee was not choosing his country — the United States, the Union — but something *opposed* to his country. Yet Lee did not think of the nation as a legal unit indivisible, a judicial entity with one National Will (that Will ordering him to fight). Nor did he justify his choice on the grounds that he had a new country, the Confederacy, established by the right of self-determination. This whole cast of thought was foreign to him — as would have been E. M. Forster's famous dictum: "I hate the idea of causes, and if I had to choose between betraying my country and betraying my friend, I hope I should have the guts to betray my country." Forster equates, in the modern manner, country with Cause. Lee did not. He was not fighting for any Cause, for slavery or the Confederacy. For him country *meant* one's friends — the bond of affection that exists among countrymen; and when a rift opened in this union of persons, he had to choose those to whom he was bound by primary rather than secondary ties….

And say not thou "My country right or wrong,"
Nor shed they blood for an unhallowed cause.

John Quincy Adams, **Congress, Slavery, and an Unjust War**, 1847.

WAR AND SELF-DEFENSE

Lee did not help his fellow Virginians because they were right, or because he approved of anything they wanted to do as a body. He joined them only when it became a choice of killing one's own, or watching them be killed, or protecting as many of them as he could at the risk of dying with them. Only at that last extremity was he edged over to their side. Ironically, those who best grasp the moral norms of the Old South's general are some of the New South's blacks. Loyal to America, convinced that their people are far better off in the larger complexus of American society, many black leaders strive to prevent division between the races; but they are forced to say candidly that, if intransigence on either side forces an insane choice upon them, they must stand with their people.

The most important aspect of Lee's choice is that, since he did not conceive of his state as a Cause, or as himself writ large, or as a Will that absorbed his, there were no grounds left for justifying war except the argument of self-defense. Killing others is justifiable if they are about to kill oneself or one's family or one's people — not to prove a point, or spread some creed by the sword. Lee has become something like a secular saint, a holy warrior in our history, because he did not fight a Holy War. Men who abominate slavery can admire him, since he did not fight for slavery — or for anything but protection of his people. It is the only honorable motive for war....

VIETNAM IS NOT OUR COUNTRY

Our country, right or wrong? — we can hardly be thinking in those terms when (as the Maryland Secretary of Health has put it) "the average American pays $402.08 a year in taxes for armaments but only $2.52 for food to feed his fellow citizens"; when we are willing to "send the gunboats" to "protect the flag" when one American citizen is threatened abroad, by foreigners, but are unwilling to think of the national prestige as engaged in the protection of American children from rats in this country's slums. The competitive ethic makes us think of any American as "on our team" when we are competing abroad, with other countries, but reduces that same American to a rival, a potential enemy, in our domestic competition, our struggles against each other in the marketplace; so that patriotism is degraded from love of countrymen to mere hatred of foes, mere xenophobia, and men consider it "patriotic" to prefer the muddled abstractions of "confrontation with Communism" in Vietnam to the lives of our young men. We no longer know what "our country" is — as Lee knew, in the tragedy of 1860, what his country was, that it what his country-*men*, his erring Virginians. We need a new, more humane concern for our country (right or wrong) — and Vietnam is not our country.

America and
the Defense of Freedom

Melvin Munn

Melvin Munn is a regular political commentator
on the Life Lines radio program. The following
reading is part of a broadcast delivered by
Munn which also was reprinted in the news-
letter Life Lines.

Consider the following questions while reading:

1. What does it mean to be an American?
2. How is America defined?
3. Who are our enemies and what do they think about
   America?

Melvin Munn, **What Being an American Should Mean**, a Freedom Talk reprint.

BEING AN AMERICAN

We hear orators speak and we read dissertations upon what it means to be an American. Let's think for a few minutes on what it should mean to every man, woman, and child in the United States to be an American.

Being an American should mean many wonderful things to you. Does it?

At the risk of being accused of preaching a bit, we would like to think with you for the next few minutes about what it ought to mean to be an American. Unfortunately there are those in our land today who place very little value on being an American — so little, in fact, that they would betray their country and destroy its government and its way of life.

Being an American ought to mean that we are proud of our history and of the heroes whose deeds of valor and service to their fellow-man are the high points in that history.

No other nation on earth has a history which will compare with ours. There are nations much older. They may have longer histories, but not nearly so filled with illustrious deeds and with the ideals of freedom which have been the foundation of our nation since colonial days.

No other nation has ever been able to afford its people either so great a measure of individual freedom and dignity or such a luxurious standard of living. We have a right to look back and to be proud of the past which has given us the blessing of today and, if preserved, the promise of a wonderful future....

The United States of America has not only met crises in her own development, but has fought to perpetuate freedom for others and to defeat aggressors seeking to enslave the world. The world looks to America as the principal bastion of freedom today because of what we have done in the past and what we have been in the past.

In the past, certainly until relatively recent years, we have known just where our leaders stood and what our policy was with regard to the rest of the world. Our nation stood foursquare and commanded respect. That, too, is part of the greatness of our history.

Being an American ought to mean many more things. It ought to mean that each of us thrills at the sight of Old Glory, that seeing the red, white, and blue rippling on the breeze has real meaning for us.

For Americans who have followed this great flag in time of national emergency — World War I, World War II, in Korea, or in Viet Nam — one need not urge reverence for the flag. They know what the flag means, and any attempt by anybody to dishonor Old Glory will bring a quick protest from a veteran. But far too many of the rest of us take Old Glory for granted. It has flown over us ever since we can remember, and we never really took to trouble to think about what it means. It is time we did consider what this symbol of our land means and just what a terrible thing it is when the flag is dishonored.

THE BEAUTY OF AMERICA

Being an American ought to mean that we love our country and that the United States means a great deal to us as individuals, along with our families and our church. Physically and geographically, this is a great land, a country blessed with wonderful natural resources, pleasant climate, and a variety of nature's greatest beauties.

What is this land we call America? It is a broad land, stretching from the stormy Atlantic to the blue Pacific and from the Great Lakes to the Gulf of Mexico and Mexico itself. It has vast green plains and valleys, blue and purple mountains rising into the sky, and mighty rivers flowing endlessly to the sea, and crystal lakes filled with shiny fish. It is towering green forests and lush fields of corn. It is seaports haunted by the blast of the freighter's horn and it is industrial cities teeming with hurry and bustle.

It is ribbons of superhighways and hundreds of airports where the giant planes thunder and roar as they land and take off. It has a great throbbing heart and great capacity for work and production. It is huge fleets of trucks and thundering trains on silver rails.

Most of all it is people — a people with a great heritage — a people born to a greatness because of what their forefathers were. It is people who love to live, who spend more time in re-creation and luxury than any people before them, but a people who can rise to meet any emergency and go forth into any battle ready to make whatever sacrifice is necessary to van-quish the enemy and win the victory. We are a people accus-tomed to winning and not ready to settle for anything less. Being an American ought to mean loving the nation and its people — for what they are....

I AM AN AMERICAN

I am an American — who gets a lump in his throat when he hears the "Star Spangled Banner" and who holds back tears when he hears those chilling high notes of the brassy trumpet when Old Glory reaches the top of the flag pole.

Alan McIntosh, Publisher, The Rock County Herald, Luverne, Minnesota, "I Am A Tired American."

PARTICIPATE IN GOVERNMENT

Being an American ought to mean that we participate in our government. The founding fathers wisely established a consti-tutional republic, in which citizens elect their representatives to make laws and to administer the affairs of state. Only when the people in general participate in their government, as intended when the Constitution was written, will the govern-ment function properly. This means we have not only a pri-vilege but a duty and a responsibility to vote and to vote in-telligently.

We should take part in party affairs and exercise a voice in formulating the party platforms. We should communicate as much as possible with our elected officials and let them know our opinions on issues which arise. Only if this is done can they represent us as they should.

We have the constitutional right to criticize acts by our govern-ment with which we do not agree, but our right to criticize skates on very thin ice if we do not participate in choosing and helping to direct government.

Americans ought to love the freedom they have as citizens of this great land. Nowhere else does the individual have so much freedom as is guaranteed under our Constitution. The objective of the Constitution, in addition to providing a framework for our government, is to protect the freedom of the individual against encroachments from the government. No other constitution is based upon such an objective.

Somehow, never having known what it was to live without these freedoms, we tend to take them for granted, and we don't realize that people in other lands do not have them.

THE COMMUNIST ENEMY

If we, then, are proud of our heritage, our history, and the heroes that helped make this nation great, if we get a real thrill at the sight of Old Glory, if we truly love our great land, and if we participate in our government and practice self-reliance, seeking to take advantage of the opportunities it affords, it follows that we should know who our enemies are.

We do have enemies. The followers of Marxism cannot stand idly by and see our great nation at work. They detest it as a bastion of freedom — opposed to the system for which they stand. Being an American means we should inform ourselves about our enemies and how they operate.

Being an American should also mean that we are willing to make whatever sacrifices may be necessary to preserve our heritage of freedom for our children. We today hold in our hands the keys to the future of this great nation. It has been well said that freedom must be rewon with every new generation, and our time of testing is now.

Pressure is growing within from those who profess to follow communism. The hordes of communists in other lands are watching with anticipation for the moment when they think our nation is ready to fall or can be overcome by military or other means.

Americans have in the past risked boldly for freedom, both for themselves and for others. Today, being an American should mean we are still willing to stand foursquare for freedom of the individual and the dignity of man.

The call today is for patriotism to be revived and love of freedom to be renewed, for in America lies the hope of man for a bright future.

Reproduced with permission of the Manchester (NH) Union Leader.

America and World Economic Exploitation

The Western Socialist

The following article appeared in *The Western Socialist*, a Marxist oriented bi-monthly journal published in Boston, Massachusetts. In it, the author depicts nationalism as a capitalist ploy aimed at the economic exploitation of other nations and ultimately benefiting America's multinational corporations.

Consider the following questions while reading:

1. How can nationalism be defined?
2. Why is the school an ideal place for fostering nationalism?
3. What is the relationship between capitalism and nationalism?

"Nationalism," **The Western Socialist**, 1970, Volume 37, pp. 13-16. Reprinted with permission.

NATIONALISM: INFANTILE AND ARCHAIC

Historically, the growth of nationalism goes back to the seventeenth and eighteenth centuries when feudal states were united to form nations. Nationalism may be defined simply as an acquired strong feeling of devotion of people toward their "own country" — its language, culture, customs and traditions, and the unification under a single government of the geographic area occupied by a people. Or it can be defined in these words which tend to bring its essentially dangerous character to the fore:

> "Members of the national unit recognize their likeness and emphasize their difference from other men...The fact of nationality is urgently separatist in character...It is exclusive and it promotes a loyalty which may often, like family affection, live its life independent of right and truth."
> (H. J. Laski, A Grammar of Politics, p. 221.)

In this contemporary world of interdependence, feelings of nationalism are decidedly immature, infantile and archaic. But since it is recognized by our rulers that nationalism remains a great political force and a powerful political reality, they unceasingly encourage their political factotums to promote and make shrewd use of it. Though our rulers, for ulterior motives, would have their wage slaves subservient to nationalism, they themselves do not personally subscribe to such idiocy as evidenced by their ramified international financial involvements. When it comes down to the nitty-gritty, they recognize but one flag — the $ flag. We refer here, of course, to the rulers — the 1.6 percent who own 80 percent of all stock — and not to the petty business man whose products cannot be exported abroad and who therefore may be a rabid nationalist, and who may actually credit his devout patriotism to ideological reasons and not to the material fact that his patriotism pays handsome dividends for him. Natonalism today, in some respects, is a hindrance to our rulers, for it serves in some measure to limit their freedom of action. They seek to by-pass their creation — nationalism — without, however, seriously weakening its emotional status in the minds of workers nor arousing their antipathy by actions which might be constructed by the latter as being unpatriotic.

NATIONALISM AND MULTINATIONAL CORPORATIONS

Former U.S. Undersecretary of State, George W. Ball, highlighted this hindrance in these words as quoted in "Business Week," February 17, 1968:

> "There is an inherent conflict of interest between corporate managements that operate in the world economy, and governments whose points of view are confined to the narrow national scene...."

According to McKinsey & Co.'s Managing Director Gilbert H. Clee, these multinational corporations, as they are called, want room "to move around the world with some degree of assurance — (government support and protection)."

As quoted in "Business Week," Ball issues this warning:

> "Conflict will increase between the world corporation, which is a modern concept evolved to meet the requirements of the modern age, and the nation-state, which is still rooted in archaic concepts unsympathetic to the needs of our complex world."

Since our rulers indirectly but none the less decisively rule the government — the state — it is a foregone conclusion that the latter will accelerate its present support of these multinational corporations in their global economic ventures. By so doing, politically, economically, and militarily, the impediments to foreign governments can be frequently overcome.

But this by no means indicates that there will be a lessening of nationalistic fostering by our rulers. Actually, nationalism will be intensified. It will take on an added hue, as it has commenced to do of late, to accommodate the ambitions of the multinational corporations.

THE END OF CAPITALISM
With the end of capitalism and the exploitation of one class by another, "the exploitation of one nation by another will also be put to an end."

The gearing of national policies and opinion in the West in support of multinational corporations has for some time been apparent in official pronouncements no less than in economic writings such as was quoted above. For instance, Eisenhower, in his state of the Union Message in 1953, defined the aims of American foreign policy as

> "doing whatever our Government can properly do to encourage the flow of private investment abroad. This involves, as a serious and explicit purpose of our foreign policy, the encouragement of a hospitable climate for such investment in foreign countries...."

PROPAGANDA IN THE SCHOOLS

The school is an ideal setting for fostering nationalism. As an agent of nationalist propaganda, it is most effective because it is general; because school attendance up to a certain age is compulsory, and because it catches the individual at an impressionable age. Its curriculum permits easy injection of nationalism. History and geography, for example, are taught from a strict national point of view, directly and indirectly: directly through emphasis on the national interest, the result of which is that the U.S.A. emerges as the finest country in the world, and indirectly by teaching history and geography at the expense of world history and world geography....

NATIONALISM, CAPITALISM AND COMMUNISM

Nationalism will slowly but surely follow the demise of the socio-economic order — capitalism — to which it owes its genesis and crystallization. Having in its rise developed nationalism, capitalism has also produced the conditions for its ultimate disintegration and disappearance. Capitalism

> "has through its exploitation of the world market given a cosmopolitan character to production and consumption in every country. To the great chagrin of reactionists, it has drawn from under the feet of industry the national ground on which it stood. All old-established national industries have been destroyed or are daily being destroyed. They are dislodged by new industries, whose introduction becomes a life and death question for all civilized nations, by industries that no longer

work up indigenous raw material, but raw material drawn from the remotest zones; industries whose products are consumed not only at home, but in every quarter of the globe. In place of the old wants, satisfied by the productions of the country, we find new wants, requiring for their satisfaction the products of distant lands and climes. In place of the old local and national seclusion and self-sufficiency we have intercourse in every direction, universal interdependence of nations. And as in material, so also in intellectual production. The intellectual creations of individual nations become common property. National one-sidedness and narrow-mindedness become more and more impossible, and from the numerous national and local literatures there arises a world literature.'' (''Communist Manifesto.'')

With the end of capitalism and the exploitation of one class by another, ''the exploitation of one nation by another will also be put to an end.'' With the coming of socialism and our entrance into a world without mental or physical frontiers, the capitalist created concept of nationalism with its barbaric features will be but a historic legacy found only in the dusty pages of history books.

The Need for Independence

Mrs. Wilson K. Barnes

Organized in August, 1890, the Daughters of
the American Revolution is a national society of
over seven million women dedicated to the per-
petuation of patriotic ideals in America. Its
national headquarters in Washington, D.C.
owns and operates Constitution Hall, a building
which houses a library of over forty thousand
books and twenty thousand manuscripts on
American genealogy. Mrs. Wilson K. Barnes,
Chairman of the National Defense Committee,
delivered the following address on April 18,
1961 at the Society's seventieth Continental
Congress.

Consider the following questions while reading:

1. How is world government described?
2. What is the meaning of patriotism?

Mrs. Wilson K. Barnes, ''Patriotic Principles of Americanism,'' **Vital Speeches**, June 1, 1961,
p. 497. Reprinted with permission.

WE MUST REMAIN STRONG

The greatest good that our country can do the free nations of the world is to be and remain strong, spiritually, militarily, and materially. Here, upon this soil, because of freedom from regulation, our ancestors carved out of the very wilderness itself, without foreign aid, a great empire built upon the principles of freedom, equality, and justice. Our Government was proclaimed to be a government of the people, by the people, and for the people, whose just powers were derived from the consent of the governed. This freedom, so dearly bought, was not won in a day but the lessons learned in its winning should be instilled in those who would claim the right to nationhood. Freedom cannot be bought; it must be earned....

WORLD GOVERNMENT IMPERILS FREEDOM

It is easy to believe in world government. The human heart yearns for peace and surcease from the troubles that beset us. How wonderful it would be to wake up one morning and be told that war would be no more. That one could travel freely from one end of the world to the other. That the imprisoned nations of the earth were again free. That our children could plan their lives and all people everywhere fulfill their yearned-for aspirations. This promise was as nearly fulfilled as anywhere in the world in these United States, because our people knew the secret of freedom — a system of checks and balances, knowing well that that government is best which governs least. The character of a world government, represented today in essence by the United Nations, is reactionary — a return to absolutism and totalitarianism so abhorred by those who for generations have fled from the tyrannical governments of the Old World. There is nothing to check the absolute power of world government, its decrees, its judgments; its legislative acts are final. Nations such as Soviet Russia do not abide by United Nations decrees except when it suits them...but nations who live by moral standards seek to abide by its regulations. Thus, we have noted that the United States picked up the tabs for the international police force and is contributing large sums for the Congo.

Americans who understand the foundations upon which liberty was erected realize that a world order is the greatest enemy of individual freedom, not a means to achieve it. True freedom depends on local self-Government, on effective access of the people to their individual rights and not on a distant and powerful world Government. The heirs of Washington, Jefferson, and Lincoln know that society is improved by the individuals who compose it, not by forcing a program of social reform down its throat....

Within the Declaration of Independence, the Constitution, and Bill of Rights lies the greatness of our past and hope for the future. These great documents encompass the rules and regulations of human happiness. Americans should read and study them, understand and live by them. Let us declare our independence from a pseudophilanthropic Government. Let us recapture the knack of being Americans. Then our people will labor for what they want, experience a pride of accomplishment and feel a security which centralized social insurance cannot supply....

PATRIOTISM IS INDISPENSABLE

The present decline of American patriotism clearly requires a reversal. When a patriotic citizenry disappears, a country is done for. Patriotism is absolutely indispensable to the survival of a political sovereign power.

Christianity Today, June 7, 1974.

THE NEED FOR PATRIOTISM

Some people say it is controversial to be patriotic; if that is so, then we need more controversy in America. Some say it is sentimental to express love of country; then we need more sentimentality. Some say it is old fashioned to respect the American flag, and if that is true, we have a great need for more old-fashioned people in the United States.

The active enemies of freedom in our country probably number no more than 2 percent of the population. And yet, by constant, crafty effort, they have planted the idea far and wide that there is something a little funny about any outward show of patriotism.

We do not hear the national anthem and other patriotic songs on the air very often. We rarely witness mass recitals of the pledge of allegiance to the flag on occasions where nothing could be more appropriate. We do not find nearly enough patriotic programs on radio and television — although our adversaries have no difficulty in getting their ideas aired. We hear that some patriotic programs we have enjoyed in the past find there is no longer a place for them.

We are wrong — dead wrong — to let the active opponents frighten or ridicule us away from demonstrations of our patriotism. Every American should have a feeling of pride in his heart at any opportunity to tell the world how he feels about this land of the free.

This is the country, let us remember with deep gratitude that gave first consideration to the individuality of man, his hunger for freedom, his faith in himself and his God, and his desire for the expression of this divinely endowed impulse. It is a proud and joyful thing to be an American, and Americans should take pride and joy in expressing their patriotism.

Here is what we must say: "You shall not take our freedom away. Nor shall you, by mockery or deceit, cause us to hesitate to take the course of thinking right — talking right — for America."

Our ancestors produced a great Republic. Let us keep it.

Viewpoint 21

The Need for Interdependence

Luther H. Evans

A PhD from Stanford University, Luther H.
Evans has had a long and varied association
with international peace groups. From 1953 to
1958 he was Director General of UNESCO. In
1966, he was Chairman of the Executive Committee of the Commission to Study the Organization of Peace. Since 1971, he has served as
president of the World Federalists, USA. He is
a joint author of *The Decade of Development:
Problems and Issues* (1966) and the sole author
of *The United States and UNESCO* (1971). A
committed internationalist, Evans sees nationalism as a dangerous and archaic hindrance to
world peace.

Consider the following questions while reading:

1. Why are there so many problems in world affairs?
2. How can countries of the world best solve their problems?
3. What is needed in the United States?

Luther Evans, ''What the World Needs: A Real Peace Movement,'' **The Humanist**, July/
August 1975, pp. 14-16. This article first appeared in **The Humanist** July/August 1975 and is
reprinted by permission.

A BAD SITUATION

Seldom in modern times has the management of world affairs been in such a mess as it is today, and seldom have the world's peoples been so frustrated and dispirited. Not many individuals or groups see a way out, and governments not only do not realize the perils their people are in but also lack the skill or the will to do much about it. When they do recognize an individual peril, they (or at least the big nations) generally think of national security, which means almost anything they can persuade or delude their people that it means. They also are willing to use economic power and the threat of violence to assure their people that they are not to be the last to get the spoils in a disintegrating world....

Why are we in this mess? It is mainly because governments feel themselves to be adversaries, and because the principles by which their adversary relations are governed lack morality and constancy. Governments frequently mouth the rhetoric of peace and interdependence, but they really believe it only to a very limited degree, and practice even such weak belief hardly at all....

In nation-states, which have flourished during the last four to five hundred years, the principle has been basic that governments and their peoples (in countries where the people mean anything) become inheritors of the divine right of kings to do whatever they wish, in the supposed interest of the people. They believe it to be moral to conquer, to make war for good or bad reasons, to exploit colonial peoples by military, economic, or other force, to educate them for slavery or servility for their own gain or to satisfy their own prejudices, and to take advantage of other nations' situations of weakness to increase their own strength. In this work-of-the-devil they feel free to use horrendous deceit, double-dealing, breaches of faith, and other tricks of criminality to achieve and to hold power and gain supposed glory....

[A] weakness of this sort of approach is that its measure of power is mostly in military terms, and it results in repression of demands for justice, for equality, and for minority rights and self-determination. It inevitably results in arms races, secrecy, deceit, hoodwinking of the public, extremist nationalistic propaganda, more or less suppression of civil liberties (particularly freedom of speech and of the press) and of strong political opposition and, hence, of democratic tendencies, thus separating governments from their respective peoples or making the people as immoral as their government.

Powerful interests become attached to the arms industry, and as armaments grow they become more entrenched. In the absence of countervailing government pressure, labor develops a strong interest in maintaining armaments and puts pressure on its leaders to increase them or fight their reduction. Churches cannot survive well in noncommunist states without the approval of wealthy segments of the population, and hence become (in most cases) allies of nationalistic forces. Education becomes the transmission belt for current doctrines, including myths.

It is clear that the peoples of the world have absorbed the errors of their governments to a considerable degree (less perhaps in more-democratic states than in those without strong democratic traditions). The sharing of doctrines of immorality or lack of realism tends to increase with success or with combat, and decrease with defeat or failures of policy. They also increase with the growing dependence of other nations on one's favors.

CLEAR STREAM OF REASON

Where the clear stream of reason has not lost its way into the
    dreary desert sand of dead habit;
Where the mind is led forward by thee into ever-widening
    thought and action —
Into that heaven of freedom, my Father, let my country awake.

Rabindranath Tagore, ''Gitanjali.''

INTERDEPENDENCE: A POSSIBLE SOLUTION

What is needed to get out of this mad chaos? The first move is to return to the road of reason and morality. The first step on that road is to strengthen such fragments of a realization of interdependence that have been accepted by most nations. One

of these is international law, particularly the degree of world
constitutional law that we possess in the United Nations and in
such regional governmental structures as the Organization of
American States. Then we need to strengthen the sense of
world community in institutions that manage certain aspects of
world affairs, such as the equitable distribution of food, the
codification and ratification of the law of the seas, the protection of the environment, the provision of access to natural and
other basic resources, the regulation of relations between
multinational enterprises and governments, and the improvement of the monetary system and trade relations....
How do convinced believers act in order to have national
policies conform to the demands of the interdependence of
peoples? Of course, education and research and information
are of vital importance. I believe, however, that in this country

ONE SHRINKING WORLD!

Justus in the **Minneapolis Star**. Reprinted with permission.

and in many others we have enough information and research findings available to begin to save the world. There will always be a need for more education and more communication, but I believe the greatest and most important need today is to mobilize politically the informed opinion that already exists. Mobilization obviously includes communication that conveys accurate, well-researched information and educates. As concerned citizens become active as a lobby for a new conception of the national interest in solving world issues, I have no doubt that research and education will be stimulated to play the necessary supporting roles. But it is political action that will give direction to the so-called peace movement, which I define as the movement to be intelligent rather than short-sighted in protecting the national and world interest.

It is clear that a large body of opinion exists in this country and in many others in support of national policies that take account of world interdependence. Many members of Congress are working to try to hold back the tide of nationalistic reactions to international developments that people do not like. But they feel that they do not have an active citizens group supporting them. The same is true of the administration in Washington on some issues. Periodic mobilizations of opinion on certain issues in recent years demonstrate what can be done: Congress was moved forward on funding the International Development Association, on the Rhodesian Chrome sanctions issue, on the slowdown of certain weapons systems, on certain law-of-the-sea issues, on the food issue, and on international action regarding the environment — all by pressure groups working for a more enlightened concept of national interest.

UNITED STATES' RESPONSIBILITY

What we need in this country and others is a permanent and very active lobby conceived in terms of interdependence. The world is interdependent in many ways, and policies to deal with the problems arising from interdependence are themselves interdependent in so many ways that episodic lobbies on individual issues will not serve the purpose. We must see world affairs as a whole and strive for the adoption of principles of morality and world management that recognize such unity.

If we could develop such a lobby in this country, I believe many other countries would follow with similar action. Indeed, the public in several countries seems to me to be more world-minded than the American public.

Today we must look at the problem of achieving world peace and welfare as a sociological process, including a large portion of economics. The lawmaking and law-enforcement formula is simply not good enough, and besides it presumes decisions by governments and peoples that will not be made until a lot of other problems are satisfactorily dealt with. Most intelligent managers and democratic leaders would deem it irrational today to endow the United Nations with vastly more powers than it has or to abolish the veto in the Security Council. The United Nations is very imperfect, but common sense tells us that this country should be the first, rather than be among the laggards, in efforts to strengthen it step by step as opportunity offers or can be created. There are important opportunities today to do this, and we should push our government hard to make the most of them. The kind of petulance exhibited recently in some governmental and other quarters won't do. There is much in the world to be petulant about, but such reactions represent a denial of a management responsibility. Without the strong assertion and intelligent execution of our planetary management responsibility, our national interest and the world interest will be further jeopardized — and world survival perhaps imperiled. A strong lobby for interdependence would help.

Exercise 4

Distinguishing Primary From Secondary Sources

Instructions

A rational person must always question his various sources of information. Scholars, for example, usually distinguish between **primary sources** (eyewitness accounts) and **secondary sources** (writings based on primary or eyewitness accounts, or other secondary sources). A diary written by a Civil War veteran, about the Civil War, is one example of a primary source. In order to be a critical reader one must be able to recognize primary sources. This, however, is not enough. Eyewitness accounts do not always provide accurate descriptions. Historians may find ten different eyewitness accounts that interpret an event differently. They must then decide which of these accounts provide the most objective and accurate interpretations. Also remember that primary sources are not always better than secondary sources. Frequently secondary sources will prove accurate, while primary sources can be unreliable.

Test your skill in evaluating sources by participating in the following exercise. Pretend you are living 2000 years in the future. Your teacher tells you to write an essay about the causes of the nuclear arms race between 1970 and 1980. First, consider carefully each of the following sources and locate the **primary** (eyewitness) accounts. Second, rank **all** sources by assigning the number (1) to the source you think might be the most objective and accurate. Assign the number (2) to the next most accurate and so on until the ranking is finished. See if you can find any secondary sources that might be better than a primary source.

Since most sources cited below are fictitious, you cannot read and judge their accuracy. You will, however, recognize some of the people mentioned. You must guess about how their frame of reference and political views might influence perceptions of the nuclear arms race. The activity is designed to help you begin exploring the kind of source analysis needed for intelligent and rational thinking about social issues. Assume that all of the following sources deal with the broad problem of the nuclear arms race. Discuss and compare your source evaluations with other class members.

a. A diary written by Gerald Ford while he was President.

b. A tape recorded interview in 1977 with Leonid Brezhnev.

c. A book written by President Carter during his first term.

d. A television documentary produced and shown in 1985.

e. An essay written during the presidential campaign of 1976 by Senator Robert Dole, a conservative republican from Kansas.

f. A magazine article written in 1975 by Senator Walter Mondale, a liberal democrat from Minnesota.

Selected Bibliography

NINETEENTH CENTURY NATIONALISM

Karl W. Deutsch

Nationalism and Social Communication: An Inquiry into the Foundations of Nationality. Cambridge: Technology Press, 1953.

Carleton J. H. Hayes

The Historical Evolution of Modern Nationalism. New York: Richard R. Smith, 1931.

Georg Wilhelm Friedrich Hegel

Lectures on the Philosophy of History. Translated by J. Sibree, London: G. Bell and Sons, 1890.

Hans Kohn

Nationalism and Realism: 1852-1879. New York: Van Nostrand Reinhold Company, 1968.

Nationalism: Its Meaning and History. New York: Van Nostrand Reinhold Company, 1965.

The Age of Nationalism. New York: Harper and Brothers, 1962.

Prophets and Peoples: Studies in Nineteenth Century Nationalism. New York: Macmillan, 1946.

Lord Acton

Essays on Freedom and Power. Glencoe, Illinois: The Free Press, 1948.

Jules Michelet

Historical View of the French Revolution, from its Earliest Indications to the Flight of the King in 1791. Translated by C. Cocks, London: G. Bell and Sons, 1890.

TWENTIETH CENTURY NATIONALISM

America

Rustin on Black Nationalism. February 8, 1969. p. 152.

Ebony

Unity of Blackness. 24, (August 1969): 42-43.

A. Johnson

Nationalism in the Middle East. *School and Society*, September 29, 1956, p. 111.

E. S. Munger

South Africa: Are There Silver Linings? *Foreign Affairs*, 47, (January 1969): 375-386.

P. Schrag

New Black Myths. *Harper*, 238, (May 1969): 37-42.

J. Vorster

South Africa's Side of the Story. *U.S. News and World Report*, July 15, 1968, pp. 78-81.

Jamal Mohammed Ahmad

The Intellectual Origins of Egyptian Nationalism. New York: Oxford University Press, 1960.

George Antonius

The Arab Awakening: The Story of the Arab Nationa Movement. Philadelphia: Lippincott, 1939.

Salo W. Baron

Modern Nationalism and Religion. New York: Harper, 1947.

Delmar M. Brown

Nationalism in Japan. Berkeley: University of California Press, 1961.

Donald M. Brown

The Nationalist Movement: Indian Political Thought from Ranade to Bhave. Berkeley: University of California Press, 1961.

William Curt Buthman

The Rise of Integral Nationalism in France. New York: Columbia University Press, 1939.

Oscar I. Janowsky

Foundations of Israel. New York: D. Van Nostrand Company, 1959.

Nationalities and Minorities. New York: Columbia University Press, 1945.

Elie Kedourie

Nationalism in Asia and Africa. New York: The New American Library, 1970.

Hans Kohn

Pan-Slavism: Its History and Ideology. New York: Vintage Books, 1960.

Arthur P. Whitaker

Nationalism in Latin America: Past and Present. Gainesville: University of Florida Press, 1962.

AMERICAN NATIONALISM

America Nationalism Here and Abroad. October 27, 1956, p. 92.

J. Atkins Thanksgiving, U.S.A. *Readers Digest*, 103, (November 1973): 139-140.

B. Atkinson Flagwaving. *New Republic*, February 14, 1970, pp. 13-14.

W. F. Buckley Decline of Patriotism. *National Review*, November 10, 1972, pp. 1266-1267.

Christian Century Beyond Nationalism. July 3, 1957, pp. 813-814.

Commonweal After Vietnam. May 23, 1975, pp. 131-132.

Problem of Patriotism. March 8, 1968, pp. 671-672.

H. Donovan America and the World Out There. *Time*, May 19, 1975, pp. 19-20.

B. Graham Unfinished Dream. *Christianity Today*, July 31, 1970, pp. 20-21.

R. Nader We Need a New Kind of Patriotism. *Life*, July 9, 1971, p. 4.

D. Seim & G. Logsdon Why We Fly the Flag: Its My Country Too. *Farm Journal*, 95, (July 1971): 19-20.

Time Whatever Happened to Patriotism? Essay, November 10, 1967, pp. 30-31.

Merle E. Curti *The Roots of American Loyalty*. New York: Columbia University Press, 1946.

Hans Kohn *American Nationalism*. New York: Macmillan, 1957.

Albert K. Weinberg *Manifest Destiny: A Study of Nationalist Expansionism in American History*. Baltimore: Johns Hopkins Press, 1935.

133

GENERAL

I. Beslin — Bent Twig: A Note on Nationalism. *Foreign Affairs*, 51, (October 1971): 11-30.

Catholic World — Holy Father Condemns Exaggerated Nationalism. 147, (September 1938): 747-748.

Commonweal — Challenge of Nationalism. August 31, 1956, pp. 529-530.

W. H. Donaldson — Challenges of an Interdependent World. *Department of State Bulletin*, March 25, 1974, pp. 289-294.

J. N. Irwin, II — Imperative of Interdependence. *Department of State Bulletin*, December 18, 1972, pp. 697-702.

Nationalism and the U.N. *U.S. Department of State Bulletin*, May 26, 1958, pp. 872-880.

H. Kohn — Nationalism: Is it Good or Bad? *Foreign Policy Bulletin*, October 15, 1957, pp. 17-18.

H. Morgenthau — Paradoxes of Nationalism. *Yale Review*, 46, (June 1957): 81-96.

R. A. Norem — Is the Nation-State Obsolete? *Christian Century*, October 6, 1937, pp. 226-228.

J. V. Schall — Does a Bell Toll for the Nation-State? *America*, August 7, 1971, pp. 59-63.

Friedrich O. Hertz — *Nationality in History and Politics: A Study of the Psychology and Sociology of National Sentiment and Character*. Oxford: Clarendon Press, 1944.

Boyd C. Shafer — *Nationalism: Myth and Reality*. New York: Harcourt, Brace, 1955.

Louis L. Snyder — *The Meaning of Nationalism*. New York: Greenwood Press, 1968.

The Editor

BRUNO LEONE received his B.A. (Phi Kappa Phi) from Arizona State University and his M.A. in history from the University of Minnesota. A Woodrow Wilson Fellow (1967), he is currently an instructor at Metropolitan Community College, Minneapolis, where he has taught history, anthropology, and political science. In 1974-75, he was awarded a Fellowship by the National Endowment for the Humanities to research the intellectual origins of American Democracy.

SERIES EDITORS

GARY E. McCUEN received his A.B. degree in history from Ripon College. He also has an M.S.T. degree in history from Wisconsin State University in Eau Claire, Wisconsin. He has taught social studies at the high school level and is co-originator of the *Opposing Viewpoints Series*, *Future Planning Game Series*, *Photo Study Cards* and *Opposing Viewpoints Cassettes*. He is currently working on new materials to be published by Greenhaven Press.

DAVID L. BENDER is a history graduate from the University of Minnesota. He also has an M.A. in government from St. Mary's University in San Antonio, Texas. He has taught social problems at the high school level and is a co-originator of the *Opposing Viewpoints Series*, *Future Planning Game Series*, *Photo Study Cards* and *Opposing Viewpoints Cassettes*. He is currently working on new materials that will be published by Greenhaven Press.